Pop a Smoke

Pop a Smoke

*Memoir of a Marine
Helicopter Pilot in Vietnam*

RICK GEHWEILER

McFarland & Company, Inc., Publishers
Jefferson, North Carolina

Library of Congress Cataloguing-in-Publication Data

Names: Gehweiler, Rick, 1944– author.
Title: Pop a smoke : memoir of a Marine helicopter pilot in Vietnam /
    Rick Gehweiler.
Description: Jefferson, North Carolina : McFarland & Company, Inc.,
    Publishers, 2022 | Includes index.
Identifiers: LCCN 2022017619 | ISBN 9781476688640
    (paperback : acid free paper) ∞
    ISBN 9781476646916 (ebook)
Subjects: LCSH: Gehweiler, Rick, 1944- | Vietnam War, 1961-1975—
    Aerial operations, American. | United States. Marine Corps. Medium
    Helicopter Squadron 362—Biography. | Vietnam War, 1961-1975—Personal
    narratives, American. | Helicopter pilots—United States—Biography. |
    Helicopter pilots—Vietnam—Biography. | Youngstown (N.Y.)—Biography. |
    BISAC: HISTORY / Wars & Conflicts / Vietnam War
Classification: LCC DS558.8 .G45 2022 |
    DDC 959.704/3092 [B]—dc23/eng/20220420
LC record available at https://lccn.loc.gov/2022017619

British Library cataloguing data are available

ISBN (print) 978-1-4766-8864-0
ISBN (ebook) 978-1-4766-4691-6

On the cover: Rick Gehweiler in the cockpit, 1969; H-34 Sikorsky helicopter
(USMC Combat Helicopter Tiltrotor Association)

Printed in the United States of America

McFarland & Company, Inc., Publishers
  Box 611, Jefferson, North Carolina 28640
  www.mcfarlandpub.com

To all those who served in the Vietnam War
and the 58,200 American service men and women
who lost their lives in that effort.

To the 40,000 helicopter pilots who served
in the Vietnam War and the 4,877 pilots
and crew members who lost their lives in that effort.

To all those Marines who served in HMM-362
during the Vietnam War and the 33 pilots
and air crews that lost their lives in that effort.

And the most heartfelt and sincere dedication
to my dear friend and roommate,
Ron "Hauser" Janousek, who lost his life
and was never able to come home.

Semper Fidelis

Table of Contents

Acknowledgments

It still amazes me that I had this desire to start writing so late in life. The process was significantly more difficult than I had imagined but also tremendously rewarding. I had this story I wanted to tell, perhaps for my own personal therapy as much as for others I thought might find it interesting and important. Throughout the evolution of the book, I was fortunate to have support, advice, and professional expertise, without which I could never have completed the project. I want to thank the following contributors.

Thank you to my dear cousin Larry Irwin who has always been like a brother to me. When I told Larry that I was writing a book about my Vietnam experience he asked if he could please read what I had put to paper early in the process. After he read what I sent him he was astonished at the content because I had never talked about those times to anyone. He said it was an incredible story but needed work and asked if he could help me edit what I had. Aware that I needed all the help I could get, I eagerly agreed. He made copious notes and suggestions for changes, running through a handful of red pens in the process. Through Zoom meetings and a lot of time and effort on his part we made significant progress and improved the manuscript significantly. Thanks, pal, for all your time and effort.

Thank you to the Pop A Smoke organization (USMC Combat Helicopter and Tiltrotor Association) and its current president Slick Katz (yes, that is his real name) for agreeing to allow me to use the organization name for the title of my book. Slick is a unique man in that he entered the Marine Corps as a private in 1968, serving a tour in Vietnam as a crewman on UH-1E (Huey) helicopters with HM L-167 and through his career working his way up to the officer corps, eventually attaining the rank of colonel until his retirement in 2004. No mean feat in the Marine Corps, I can assure you. Thank you, Colonel, sir.

Acknowledgments

A huge debt of gratitude and thanks to my fabulous editor Bill Greenleaf of Greenleaf Literary Services. This book would never have made it to print without him and his editorial support and expertise. After my cousin Larry and I did all that work in the trenches early on I knew I still needed a professional editor. Providence brought me to Bill. His website listed just the services I was looking for and after an initial phone call he agreed to take a look at my manuscript. His evaluation was very supportive, and he felt it had enough quality and content to perhaps be publishable. Of course, he informed me that it needed a lot of additional work to get it to that point. He gave me the option of enlisting him to do the work himself but confided in me that he felt I could do the same work under his supervision. I chose the latter approach as it gave me the opportunity to learn and improve as a writer. It was indeed a laborious task, but I did gain a measure of confidence and skills that I hope will serve me well in the future. Can't thank you enough, Bill, for all your expertise, advice, and support. I'm already working on our next project together.

A very special big heartfelt thanks to McFarland for taking on a rookie writer with a manuscript in such a narrow genre. It's hard to imagine as I write this today that my book will actually be published. I looked long and hard to find a literary agent that would be interested in representing my book, however, all the agents I contacted (more than a hundred) were not interested in this subject matter and genre. Somehow I found McFarland during my extensive search process. It was a damn fine day for me when I got their response of interest. They were tremendous at guiding me through the process of getting my manuscript prepared for submission and made me feel like I had a true partner in the effort. Their communication and direction were always prompt, informative and precise. While I did have communication with a few different representatives at McFarland as the process evolved, I want to especially thank Layla Milholen who was my principal contact at McFarland.

Finally, thanks to all my family and friends who supported my effort and gave me the confidence to complete *Pop a Smoke*, especially to my dear wife Cheryl who endured all the time I spent ensconced in my office typing away for all those months. Her support and confidence in my story and skills were crucial to my efforts. "Thank you, sweetheart. You are the best."

Preface

At seventy-seven years of age, it seems a bit late to start writing. Better late than never, I suppose. While it has taken me fifty years to get around to writing this book, I only really thought about it seriously for the last two.

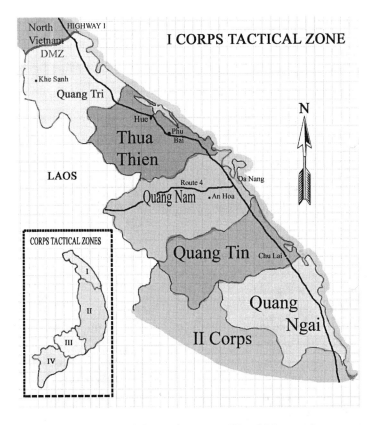

I Corps tactical map (courtesy Hotel 25vv.org).

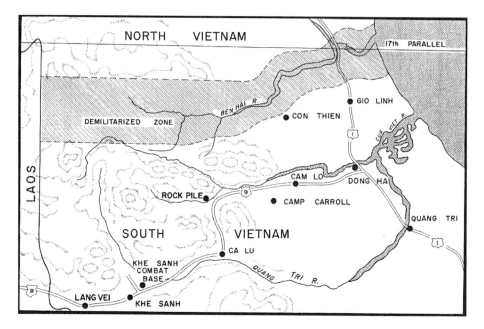

DMZ map (courtesy Hotel 25vv.org).

Originally I wanted to see if I could not only write about my experiences as a helicopter pilot in Vietnam, but more importantly, to see if I could bring the reader into the cockpit to hear, see, smell, and feel the visceral experience of flying a helicopter in a combat environment. Flying a helicopter is such a unique and exciting experience, but in combat it is an experience unlike any other. Could I create the adrenaline in the reader that I felt flying in those conditions? Could I transport the reader to that time and place?

I hope that in some measure I have done that. More importantly, I wanted to tell the story of the men I flew with and the sacrifices they made, and to tell a story of history that I feel is at risk of vanishing from the consciousness of many Americans. The story of Vietnam and those who served and died there should not be forgotten. Agreement or disagreement with the war is not the issue. Not forgetting it is.

Fifty years is a long time, and my memory of details and names has suffered. I want to emphasize that as a result of the considerable passage of time I have had to create some of the names of those men and recreate some of the incidents, conversations, and details to the best of my knowledge. While some of my tale may read like fiction the events and the people are representative of the overall real experience. Accuracy of conversations was not critical to my effort. The story was. It is not my intent to paint myself as anyone special. On the contrary, my experiences pale compared to what so many did in the service to our country. That story has to be told.

In the end, I hope the reader will feel the thrill of flying in combat and remember the importance of what those who served sacrificed.

So now, come with me ... let's go get in the cockpit of an H-34.

Rick Gehweiler (author's collection).

1

Pop Smoke

By the end of January 1969, I'd been in Vietnam three months. I was a Marine Corps helicopter pilot attached to HMM-362, a helicopter squadron known as the "Ugly Angels." Some days were routine, and others were anything but.

I'd been assigned, along with three other pilots and copilots, to resupply and medevac operations in support of 3/2, a battalion of Marines operating just south of the demilitarized zone, or DMZ, which separated North and South Vietnam. The 3/2 signified the 3rd Battalion of the 2nd Regiment in the 1st Marine Division. The division was assigned to combat operations in I Corps, which covered the area from the DMZ south to Da Nang.

We flew the Sikorsky H-34, the first model of helicopter to see duty in Vietnam. In 1962, HMM-362 became the first helicopter squadron to serve in Vietnam. It provided support to the South Vietnamese army in its fight against the Viet Cong and the North Vietnamese regulars. The squadron was called "Archie's Angels" after its commanding officer, Lieutenant Colonel Archie Clapp. A veteran of World War II and Korea, Colonel Clapp was a fearless and innovative leader. He developed tactics and support procedures that would set the standard for helicopter operations throughout the Vietnam War.

After Colonel Clapp retired, the squadron was renamed the "Ugly Angels" due to the H-34's ungainly appearance and its role as an angel of mercy for saving hundreds of lives over years of harrowing medevac missions. It became the primary support aircraft for the Marines when they entered the war as a fully operational combat force in 1965.

The bad news was that by 1969, the H-34 was an older and underpowered aircraft. It had some serious limitations, especially in the high humidity and altitude of the mountainous areas in western Vietnam and the DMZ. The good news was that it could take some significant damage and keep flying. The pilot and copilot sat side by side in the cockpit, situated above a big Wright radial 1820 reciprocating engine, which was encased by clamshell doors at the front of the aircraft. Since most ground fire came from below, the engine frequently acted as a huge bullet bouncer. Most other helicopters in the war by then had overhead jet engines and nothing more than plexiglass between the pilots and whatever fire came from below.

On rare occasions we'd land at Quang Tri for lunch. Walking to the mess hall from the flight line, we always passed a long line of combat-damaged H-46s. The plexiglass on many was damaged so badly, we knew the pilots would have been lucky to survive. I remember thinking, *Thank God I'm flying the 34, and not one of those 46s.*

It was eight-thirty on a Monday morning in February, and the operations shack was crammed with pilots and copilots awaiting their orders. The building, like all buildings at Phu Bai, was a simple rectangle with wooden walls rising three feet from a concrete pad and screening covering the rest of the expanse to the low metal roof overhead. The screening allowed for some air circulation to combat the insufferable heat of Vietnam, but that day there wasn't a whisper of a breeze. The room smelled like a gym full of old sneakers.

My copilot that day was Dave Evans, a big blond farm boy from Nebraska who had a slow and easy way about him. He'd played linebacker at the University of Nebraska and was named All-American his senior year. Square-jawed, with a generous smile and a gentle disposition, he was as nice a guy as I ever met. Dave had been in the squadron five months, and while he'd been in-country longer than I had been, it was my turn as pilot. At that point in the war, there were no more H-34 pilots being assigned to the squadron; the H-34 was being replaced by the newer H-46s. With no new copilots to train, we just rotated back and forth between pilot and copilot duties. Dave's experience was a plus and having him as my copilot was reassuring. Having a calm and steady presence in the cockpit is a must in combat.

The second aircraft on our flight of two was piloted by Skeeter Dubois. Skeeter always wore a mischievous smile, had a heavy Cajun accent, and was never at a loss for words no matter what the topic, especially if that topic was his hometown of New Orleans. "Y'all think I'm jokin' when I tell ya that N'awlins is tha best city in tha country, but I can garrontee that we got tha finest-lookin' women in tha world dare. And ain't no better food than down-home Cajun cookin'. Tha's fo' shore."

1. Pop Smoke

He was thin-framed and had a gait not unlike a chicken, his head bobbing along atop a long, skinny neck as he regaled anyone who'd listen with his impressive collection of jokes. I never saw a man who could drink as much as Skeeter. I always felt Skeeter had joined the Marines to get away from trouble at home. Men joined the Marines for a lot of reasons. Some were running to something, while others were running away from something.

His copilot that day was Ian Kelly, a stocky, freckled-faced, red-haired Irishman who had distinguished himself as captain of the boxing team before graduating from Notre Dame, and had the nose to prove it. By contrast, Ian had a wonderful tenor voice and would from time to time grace us with a beautiful rendition of "Danny Boy." An Irishman myself, I always felt moved by it. Ian was expected to join his father's law firm upon his graduation, but to his father's dismay, he'd joined the Marines to fly. His father was furious, but most people could never understand what it was that made us want to fly so much, especially combat missions. I'm not sure we really knew why either, but it was a passionate force within each of us.

By nine o'clock, we were bathed in sweat and wishing we were flying and not sitting in a sauna. At least there would be a breeze through the cockpit. Be careful what you wish for.

The orders came at nine-fifteen. Both A and C companies in the battalion were in serious contact and needed fresh troops, ammo, and medical evacuations. Dave grabbed the paperwork from the operations officer, and we headed out to our aircraft, followed by Skeeter and Ian.

I looked at Dave as we walked to our aircraft and smiled. "At least we aren't frying in that miserable sweatbox."

"Amen to that," Dave replied, as he strode along beside me in his usual farm-boy manner. He ran a hand through his damp blond hair.

The H-34s were parked in a revetment area atop what was called Marston Matting. The perforated metal plates could be linked together to form parking areas for aircraft and in some cases runways. By 9:20, you could fry an egg on them. The 34s had been sitting there all morning, and by the time we climbed into the cockpit, it was like an oven.

Dave looked over from the copilot's seat and grinned. "What was that about not frying in a miserable sweatbox?"

Adrenaline began coursing through my veins as we went through our preflight checklist. I turned on the ignition. The first cough of that

7

big radial engine is a sound unlike any other. The only comparison I can think of is four or five Harley-Davidsons starting up together. A big plume of smoke belched from the exhaust pipe just below the cockpit. The cabin filled with smoke and the unmistakable smell of fuel and oil. The combination of sounds and smells as the 34 rocked a bit side to side is a moment when a pilot becomes one with the aircraft.

The engine roared, and the old 34 shuttered and vibrated as it came to life. Once the RPMs (engine revolutions per minute) were up to speed, I engaged the rotor head, and the air filled with the high whine of the four rotor blades as they sliced through the hot morning haze. The rotor blades picked up speed, and the H-34 continued shuddering, straining to lift itself into the sky. I raised the collective lever with my left hand and stabilized us into a three-foot hover, checking our RPMs. I pressed forward slightly with my right hand on the cyclic stick between my legs, and we moved slowly forward to begin our ascent.

Helicopter pilots always like to explain that helicopters don't really fly—they just keep from crashing. Whatever the case, there's nothing more exhilarating than flying one, especially when you're headed into combat.

The adrenaline continued pulsing through me, and every sensory fiber in my body was on full alert. This was where the rubber met the road. Every bit of training and experience came into play, and I focused on what lay ahead.

In addition to the pilot and copilot, the H-34 carried a crew chief and a door gunner. Both sat in the belly of the aircraft, with its single-entry door on the right side, where the M60 machine gun was mounted. All loading and unloading happened through that right-side door, unlike the well-known Huey helicopter, which was open on both the right and left sides. The one-door configuration of the H-34 made for some significant restrictions when loading, unloading, and returning fire with the M60.

I had an experienced crew in the belly of the H-34 that day. My crew chief, already on his second tour, was Stacy Brinkman. Solid and fearless, he oversaw the mechanical integrity of the aircraft as well as all the loading and unloading on each mission. "Keg" Johnson—I never did know his real first name—was the door gunner, and I'm fairly sure his nickname came from his beer-drinking prowess. Keg was a "short-timer," near the end of his first tour.

Our two aircraft headed to the north end of the base, where the reinforcements and supplies were staged for our mission to the embattled elements of Alpha and Charlie companies.

Due to the heat and the limitations of the H-34, we could only carry four combat-ready Marines. They loaded into each of our aircraft along with medical supplies and ammo boxes. Two other 34s had already loaded and were waiting for us. We'd form two flights of two aircraft each in the support mission.

Once loaded, our two aircraft took off into the haze and heat, headed west toward the rice paddies and jungles of Vietnam. Every man has his own thoughts in these moments. I just tried to focus on the flying and what I'd need to do when we reached the LZ. A cockpit is no place for bad thoughts or uncertainty.

The *whump-whump-whump* of the helicopter rotor blades was so familiar to us by now that it was almost soothing. That sound would define the Vietnam War forever. It was as much a part of our being as our heartbeats and would remain a part of our souls forever.

As we headed west, the checkerboard of rice paddies and bordering dikes reflected the morning sun like a thousand mirrors flashing back at us. Just to the left, a lone farmer was plowing his rice field behind a big water buffalo, while several large white herons circled overhead. Next to a grove of palm trees, a small village appeared. Children played in the square as men wheeled bags of rice on bicycles to market. Minutes away was a world of chaos and death. I never was good at processing these surreal moments of contradiction. The quick change was like something out of *The Twilight Zone*. And we were about to enter that zone.

As we got within a few miles, we switched our radios over to the ground frequency to contact the company radioman and get some information on the situation. I was quickly in contact with Alpha Company 2/5, call sign Hammer.

I punched the comm key to the ground unit. "Hammer, this is Yankee Lima 13," I said, using my own call sign—military alphabet for the letters and numbers on the side of my aircraft. "We are inbound with four birds. What's your sitrep?"

The radioman's voice answered my call for a situation report. "We are in contact from the tree lines west and northwest." His voice crackled. "We have ten wounded, four severe."

"Roger that." I felt sweat running down my spine. *Here we go, baby!* I thought to myself. *Pucker factor ten!*

Both companies were pinned behind a rice paddy dike with fire coming from the trees that lined both sides. It was a deadly crossfire. The enemy had prepared the trap with precision. The situation wasn't good.

I decided the best approach would be to autorotate (drop in) from 2,500 feet rather than come in low and fast. Fast wasn't really very fast due to our limitations of weight and power. Coming in low and fast would have made us more vulnerable to the ground fire ahead.

Dropping in is always an attention-getter, even for the most experienced pilot. Basically, the pilot uses a technique that mechanically disengages the engine from the rotor head. Next, he pushes the nose of the aircraft straight down, and it drops like a rock until about three hundred feet above the ground. He then reengages the engine and makes what's hopefully a smooth power-on transition to a normal landing. Making the transition too soon or too late can mean disaster, but if it works, it's an effective way to get into a hot zone quickly and minimize your exposure to ground fire.

I keyed the comm mic to the other aircraft. "This is Yankee Lima 13. We're gonna auto-in from 2,500, and Yankee Lima 23 will follow. Yankee Lima 23, wait fifteen seconds before you initiate your descent behind me. Second flight, wait until we're out before you make your descent. I'll relay the sitrep once we're out."

"Roger that, 13," replied Skeeter in Yankee Lima 23.

"Yankee Lima 18, roger," said the second flight leader, big Lou Stephens from the Bronx.

Lou was about six-foot-four with a quiet demeanor and a big smile hidden behind a huge handlebar mustache. Getting into the H-34 cockpit wasn't easy, given it was ten feet off the ground. How Lou ever climbed up and squeezed that big frame of his into that cockpit, I'll never know. But he'd been in-country for eight months and was a well-seasoned pilot with exceptional skills. He'd need them today.

Finally, the last reply came from the second pilot in the second flight. "Yankee Lima 27, roger," John Reynolds said. John was from Las Vegas, and this was his first mission as a pilot rather than a copilot. He always taped a picture of his wife and baby daughter to the inside of the cockpit when he flew. He'd been a copilot for four months, and this was his check ride to become a certified HAC, or Helicopter Aircraft Commander. Nice first day.

I punched the comm key to Alpha Company. "Hammer, this is Yankee Lima 13. We're going to auto-in from 2,500. Pop smoke on my command. Pop the smoke behind your men. We're gonna land with the smoke between us and your men to protect the off- and on-loading. I need room to get in there. Have the most severely wounded ready for the first aircraft."

"Roger that, Yankee Lima 13!" he screamed. Heavy gunfire filled the background.

Popping smoke means setting off a smoke grenade, which gives the pilot the location of the LZ as well as a clue on wind direction. This is important for an approach into the wind. Unfortunately, it tends to alert the enemy that you're coming, and where you're going to land.

We were above the LZ. I keyed the intercom mic. "Keg, clear the M60."

Two short bursts from the door gun shook the aircraft.

"Here we go, boys," I said to my crew. "Once we're in the LZ, get those men out, and get the wounded in as quickly as possible. Stay focused." I knew I didn't need to tell them any of that, but it's critical for an aircraft commander to appear calm and in control in any situation. "Keg, when we exit the LZ, I'll be turning the aircraft to the right, which will give you a good angle to the tree lines. You hose those bastards down as we get out of there."

"Roger that, sir!"

I could tell his adrenaline was racing for a chance to fire that M60. Having the chance to return fire when you're a sitting duck offered at least some degree of retribution. Marines refer to that as "gettin' some."

We were in position. A quick flip of my wrist, and the throttle was off. I jammed the collective down, punched the nose over, and put in a bit of right rudder. Then we were free-falling toward the ground. While the crew had experienced this and was ready for it, the troops in the belly hadn't, and I could hear their shouts over the roar of the engine and the howl of the wind as we plummeted downward. I'm sure they thought we were all going to die. In training, it had been amusing. In combat, not so much. These guys were going into the shit. We were too, but we, God willing, would be flying out. They were going in for a while before they would have a chance to get out, and some wouldn't … except in black bags.

The dial on the altimeter was spinning as we hurtled downward: 2,500, 2,000, 1,500 …

"Pop smoke!" I yelled into my headset, hoping the radioman on the ground could hear me.

"Popping smoke!" he yelled.

We were at one thousand feet and still dropping like a rock. I could see the yellow smoke ahead and to the right. As we passed three hundred feet, I snapped the throttle back to full power and lifted the nose of the aircraft while I raised the collective so the full pitch of the rotor blades could chew huge hunks of air and slow our descent. It must happen in a coordinated effort, and we'd trained for it over and over. But every load has a different weight, and even the different heat and humidity of each day could affect the speed of a descent.

The roar of the big 1820 radial engine straining with all its might to weather its load was deafening. I transitioned to a hover about ten feet off the ground and moved right to get behind the smoke. I set the 34 down, and Stacy pushed the troops out. I could see the wounded about thirty yards away, awaiting their chance to board. Some were sitting, and some were on stretchers with two Navy corpsmen tending to them.

Yankee Lima 17 landed behind and to the right of me just as the

H-34 Medevac (courtesy USMC Combat Helicopter Tiltrotor Association).

1. Pop Smoke

HMM 362 Ugly Angels medevac, January 1969 (courtesy USMC Combat Helicopter Tiltrotor Association).

HMM 362 Yankee Lima 32 deploying troops (courtesy USMC Combat Helicopter Tiltrotor Association).

first rounds slammed into our bird. It's a sickening sound, and a sickening feeling. I could tell the rounds had entered below and behind me into the belly of the aircraft.

"Stacy! You okay?"

"Yessir. Those bastards missed me!"

The last Marine had debarked, and Stacy was signaling the corpsmen to bring the four critically wounded Marines to the bird. I stared ahead and spotted the last Marine who had exited the aircraft running toward the cover of the dike. He stopped all of a sudden and pitched forward into the rice paddy. *Son of a bitch!*

I radioed the second flight. "Yankee Lima 18 and 27, begin your descent. Be aware we are in heavy contact from the tree lines north and northwest. Good luck."

They'd need it.

The enemy fire intensified as they poured everything into taking out our helicopters. The Marines behind the dike poured it back in a deafening and surreal exchange. The corpsmen loaded four stretchers

H-34 resupply under fire (USMC Combat Helicopter Tiltrotor Association).

carrying the most severely wounded. The aircraft had no more room or power. Stacy and Keg stacked the stretchers in as best they could. The whole process of discharging the replacements and taking on the wounded took five minutes. It seemed like five hours. Rounds continued to chew through the air above us and the ground around us. The next salvo rocked the 34 again.

"Stacy?"

"Okay, sir. But one of the wounded took a round. He's gone."

Shit! "You secure down there?" I tried to sound calm.

"Ready."

I checked to make sure the corpsmen were clear. I could see them loading the next four wounded into Skeeter's bird behind me. "This is 13, exiting stage right," I barked into the headset to let Skeeter know what I was doing. I picked the 34 up into a hover and pushed forward twenty feet to clear him behind me. Then I kicked in right rudder, spun the bird around, and headed to the river behind the paddies and out of the LZ (Landing Zone).

As we got parallel to the tree line, Keg opened with the M60, spraying our right side. I gave it full power, nose down, and took it as low as we could go until we got enough speed to pop up over the tree line to our left and follow the riverbed until we could gain altitude.

I called to Skeeter over the radio. "Yankee Lima 23, check in."

"Right behind you, 13. Got some holes and four wounded."

I checked with the second flight. "Yankee Lima 18 and 27, check in."

From Yankee Lima 18 came big Lou Stevens' voice. "Yankee Lima 18. We are still in the zone. I can see 27 is down and on fire. They're trying to get the crew out."

Son of a bitch. "We're proceeding to the field hospital, 18, and will be back. Hang in there, Lou."

"Roger, 13," he answered.

The flight back to the field hospital took twenty minutes but seemed like forever. The crew chiefs and gunners tended to the wounded as we flew. I radioed the hospital to alert them of our wounded. Out of radio range of the LZ, I had no idea how the other crews were doing.

We landed on the medical hospital pad at Phu Bai and unloaded the wounded. We had enough gas for one more trip out to the LZ before we'd have to take time to refuel. Stacy doused the floor of the aircraft with a bucket of water to wash away some of the blood. We took off,

15

made a quick stop at the supply pad for more ammo, and headed back to the LZ.

Once in range, I was back on the radio to Alpha Company. "Hammer, this is Yankee Lima 13. What's the sitrep?"

"We got the crew from your bird out," he replied. "They're alive and being treated. Your other aircraft is airborne."

"Roger that," I replied. "Wait one." I wanted to check in with Lou. "Yankee Lima 18, this is 13. Come in." I waited but didn't hear an answer. "Yankee Lima 18, this is 13," I repeated, my heart pounding.

I heard his faint reply. "This is 18, 13. Headed to the hospital with wounded. Yankee Lima 27's crew is with the grunts but alive. Will return for more medevacs once we get these boys home."

"Roger, 18. Well done. We are inbound to the LZ." *Round two, coming up*, I thought.

About five minutes out, I radioed Skeeter in Yankee Lima 17. "Skeeter, everything okay?"

"Yeah, Rick, we're good."

I noted Skeeter's serious attitude. No more joking around. We were all wired on adrenaline, getting ready for the next drop into the zone.

"Skeeter, we're going to take the same approach as before. I'll load the crew from Yankee Lima 27, and you grab some wounded."

"Roger that, 13."

I keyed the mic for Hammer. "Hammer, this is Yankee Lima 13. We are inbound to the LZ with ammo and will be on the ground shortly. Have the crew from Yankee Lima 27 ready to load onto my aircraft. Yankee Lima 17 will take on wounded. Copy?"

"Copy that, 13," came the reply, the staccato of gunfire in the background.

Just as we were positioning over the LZ, we heard fixed-wing aircraft in communication with Hammer. "This is Iron Fist with two F-4s about three minutes out," they reported. "Where do you want the ordnance?" While we'd been gone, the battalion apparently had called for air support from Chu Lai, which was only a short hop to the south.

"Iron Fist," Hammer replied, "the tree line to our west is the first target. The tree line to our northwest is the second."

"Roger, Hammer. Tell your boys to keep their heads down for a minute."

I radioed Skeeter. "Yankee Lima 17, we're going to hold our position at 2,500 until those F-4s do their thing. We'll insert after the last pass."

"Roger, 13," Skeeter replied. "Hope they fry those bastards."

A fully loaded F-4 is an awesome weapon. Just the sound of one streaking overhead at five hundred feet is enough to drop you to your knees. It's like a cannon going off. On more than one occasion, I'd been on the ground when one of these aircraft was on a run. If you knew what direction they were coming from, you could, if you looked really hard, see a black dot approaching at a tremendous speed. Before you could focus, the dot became a baseball, and then *boom*, it was overhead and gone. And that was *without* dropping ordnance.

As we circled the LZ, I could just make out the silhouettes of the F-4s approaching from the south. The first F-4 dropped what appeared to be two five-hundred-pound bombs on the first tree line, obliterating everything in an avalanche of fire and smoke. Secondary explosions from the enemy ordnance added to the surreal destruction. As he pulled up sharply, the second F-4 pilot straddled the second tree line, dropping two large tanks of napalm. The fireball extended perhaps a quarter of a mile long and five hundred feet upward. Nothing could survive it. Both tree lines were engulfed in fire and smoke.

As the second F-4 pulled up, I radioed Skeeter. "Yankee Lima 17, we're dropping in."

"Roger, 13." Even Skeeter was at a loss for words at what we'd witnessed.

No need for popping smoke on this approach. The inferno below gave us all the wind direction we needed. Once again, I chopped the power, disengaged the rotor head, pushed the nose over, kicked in a little right rudder, and began the freefall. At about three hundred feet, I rapped back the power, raised the nose, and brought the big old beast into a hover. We set down almost exactly where we'd landed earlier.

This time, there was virtually no enemy fire. The heat from the burning tree lines was intense and sent heavy smoke over us. The rotor blades caused the smoke to swirl around in a blinding cloud so thick it was difficult to make out where the wounded were being staged. An intense orange glow from the fires pulsated through the swirling white cloud, carrying what I realized was the smell of burning flesh. The sights and smells of that moment are indelibly locked in my memory.

Skeeter's voice jogged me back to reality. "Yankee Lima 17 is behind and to your right," he called through the radio, knowing I might not be able to see him.

"Roger that, 17." I keyed the intercom mic again. "Stacy, kick those ammo boxes out and look out for the crew from Yankee Lima 27." Then I called the ground crew. "Hammer, this is Yankee Lima 13. Can't see much, so get that flight crew onto my bird and any additional wounded onto the second aircraft."

"Yessir," came the reply.

Four figures in flight suits and flight helmets jogged out of the swirling orange cloud and clambered into the belly of the 34.

Stacy's voice came over the intercom. "Loaded and ready, sir."

"Hammer, we're departing, and two more birds are inbound to receive wounded."

"Yes, sir. And thank you, sir."

I radioed the 34s still holding overhead to begin their descent. The wind shifted just enough to give me some bearings, and I radioed Skeeter. "Yankee Lima 13 is exiting stage right."

"Right behind you, 13."

I picked the 34 up into a hover, made sure we had enough power for a safe departure, pushed forward again to clear Skeeter, and turned the aircraft to the right to gain a few more RPMs. I pushed the heavily loaded bird forward, gaining a little speed and lift, and once again we headed for the cover of the riverbed to the east and back to the field hospital at Phu Bai.

We set down twenty minutes later. The crew from Yankee Lima 27 clambered out, turned, and gave me a thumbs-up and a salute. I'd learn later that evening they were battered and bruised, but otherwise not too bad. Good enough to fly the next day.

We took off again, headed for the fuel dump, where we took on a half tank. We never topped off the gas tanks in Vietnam because we couldn't afford the extra weight. A helicopter's performance is depleted by heat, humidity, and altitude. While we were at low altitude in the current situation, the heat and humidity were significant. The supply loads we carried were maxing out the old 34s. Each approach and departure meant basically flying on the edge of the flight envelope. Any small mistake could mean disaster. Thankfully, our pilots were terrific, and could handle whatever was required.

We loaded up with food, water, and medical supplies, and headed back to the LZ. Our earlier trips had evacuated all the wounded. Our next mission was to deliver supplies and then what was always a tough chore mentally—to return the bodies of the Marines who'd lost their lives in battle. There are three classes of medevac missions: emergency, routine, and permanent routine. The last refers to the removal of those killed in action (KIA).

We came into the LZ on a normal approach pattern. The fighting was over. No need for subterfuge. As we approached, I radioed Hammer to pop a smoke grenade to verify the wind direction. Even though there was still smoke coming from the tree lines, I wanted to make sure the wind direction at the LZ was the same. All approaches must be made into the wind to achieve maximum lift. A downwind approach with weight is a recipe for disaster.

"Hammer, this is Yankee Lima 13. We're approaching the LZ from the east. We're carrying supplies and will onload the KIAs. Pop smoke."

Yellow smoke curled up from the LZ. The wind direction hadn't changed, and we made a smooth landing in the same spot as earlier. While the ground crew helped Stacy off-load the supplies, I looked around. To my right, through the dust and swirling yellow smoke, I could see Marines carrying stretchers loaded with black body bags.

The moment they were loaded aboard was always tough. There wasn't much time to think about it then, but later that night and for years afterward, the sight and the odor of those bodies still came to my mind. I'll never, ever forget it.

Yankee Lima 27 had been replaced by another bird and crew. Our four aircraft performed the same mission. Altogether, we'd evacuated 18 dead and 45 wounded. It was a brutal day for the battalion. The enemy had suffered somewhere between 250 and 300 KIAs, and an unknown number of wounded.

The numbers might look good on the spreadsheets at headquarters, but they were little solace to the Marines who had lost their friends, and the families who had lost their sons and brothers. Casualties are, of course, an inevitable cost of war. Those words, no matter how true, are always difficult to connect with the up-close-and-personal experience of the carnage of war, and the emotion of the losses endured.

Once back at Phu Bai, we parked our birds and climbed onto the blistering hot steel tarmac. We were bathed in sweat from the heat and the ordeals of the day. I took off my helmet, shook hands with my copilot, Dave Evans, and slapped his back. Dave had handled the flying to and from the LZ to give me a break from the intense moments of the mission.

"Great work today, pal," I told him.

"No, the great work came from you, Rick. You're one hell of a pilot. I'll fly with you anytime."

I walked around the aircraft and gave Stacy and Keg a snap salute and shook their hands. "Damn well done, boys," I said. "Get some rest." I knew full well they'd head to the NCO tent, slam a few beers, and return to the aircraft. They'd spend most of the night going over every inch, performing whatever maintenance necessary to make that 34 ready for the next day.

After debriefing in the operations shack, I made my way to my hooch. I stripped off my soaked flight suit and collapsed onto my cot. I was physically and emotionally exhausted. After a long moment, I wrapped myself in a towel and grabbed my toiletry kit.

The shower building was just down the path from my hooch. The building was the standard-size rectangle, fifty feet by twenty-two feet, with a concrete floor and walls, then the foot of screening at the top. Metal-encased lights dangled from the exposed wooden trusses that supported the tin roof. A line of simple showerheads protruded from the concrete wall on each side. A small wooden bench and towel hook separated each shower space.

I turned on the cold-water valve, and the water rushed down from the large, raised water tank next to the building. Due to the heat, the water was never really cold. I placed my hands on the wall, leaned in, and let the water wash over me. Standing under the tepid water for the better part of a half hour, I reflected on how tough the day had been for everyone, and how so many of us had cheated death once again.

It had been only three months since I'd arrived in Vietnam, and I was coming to grips with the reality that I probably wouldn't survive my full tour. Knowing the future might be short, my thoughts drifted to how I'd gotten there.

2

The Beginning

In June 1967, I was about to graduate from the University of North Carolina. I wasn't sure what I'd do with myself after that. My mother had raised me alone, and while I had a great extended family of aunts, uncles, and cousins, I didn't have a father around to advise and mentor me. That meant I had to figure out much about life on my own. While I always felt I was a little behind the curve on what my friends knew. I'd later find there was an advantage in having to be self-reliant. But at that point in life, I had neither direction nor confidence. I looked up to an uncle who was a three-star Navy admiral. Looking back, I'm sure it was my admiration and respect for him, and the confidence he demonstrated, that helped me decide to join the service.

I called Mom from school and told her of my decision.

"Ricky, are you sure this is what you want? I'm proud that you'd want to do this, but it's a big decision, and I want you to be sure about it."

"Yes, Mom, I'm sure. The more I think about it, the more sure I am."

"Well, I think you should talk to Uncle Dick before you make a final decision."

"I'm going to call him today."

"Call me back after you do."

My call to my uncle went as expected.

"Rick, if this is what you want, I couldn't be more proud or excited for you. You'll gain and learn more than you realize, and I'm sure you'll never regret your choice."

"Thanks, Uncle Dick. I'll keep you posted." I hung up and called Mom. "Uncle Dick gave me his support, so I guess that means I'm going to join."

"Well, I'm nervous, but proud. As long as you're sure."

"I'm sure. I'm excited."

Pop a Smoke

I went to the Navy recruiting office in Chapel Hill, North Carolina, the following day. The office was in a two-story, colonial-style brick building typical of the campus. This building also housed recruiting offices for the other branches of the military as well as the university ROTC program.

I walked through the big white double doors, and down the polished marble hallway. I passed the Army, Air Force, and Coast Guard offices, feeling confident in my choice of the Navy. I sensed I was about to enter a different world, much bigger and more important than I'd ever thought possible. Then I was standing in front of the door. The U.S. Navy seal covered the whole upper portion. I stood for a moment and stared.

Are you sure about this, Rick? I thought to myself. *It's a long-term, no-turning-back commitment.*

I opened the door and walked inside.

Two desks stood side by side next to some filing cabinets and a small conference table. Pictures of naval ships and planes adorned the walls along with several recruiting posters. Sitting behind the desk directly in front of me was an ensign dressed in a crisp white officer's uniform. A few ribbons were pinned above his left shirt pocket. Above the right was a black name tag that read *Saunders.* Behind his desk sat a picture of President Johnson bracketed by the U.S. and Navy flags. To the left of Ensign Saunders was a second desk manned by a petty officer also dressed in a starched white summer uniform. He had three rows of ribbons and a name tag that read *Despain.* He obviously had more time in the Navy than Ensign Saunders.

I was understandably nervous and slightly intimidated in the strange environment, but I looked at the ensign and his uniform, and I thought, *Man, this guy looks sharp.* I could see myself in that uniform. I walked up to his desk.

"Good morning," the ensign said. "What can we do for you?"

"Well, I want to join the Navy and become an aviator." I managed to get the words out with only a little tremor in my voice.

"I see. What's your name, and why do you want to join the Navy?"

"My name is Rick Gehweiler. I have an uncle who's an admiral in the Navy whom I greatly admire, and I've always wanted to fly. I'm about to graduate, and I'm not really sure what I want to do. I think the Navy would be a good opportunity for me to grow."

"Okay, Mr. Gehweiler, have a seat," Ensign Saunders said. He produced a packet of paperwork from his desk. "Once you've looked through all of this and filled out the necessary paperwork, return tomorrow at 0900, and we'll give you some tests." The military time of 0900 means 9:00 a.m.

I returned the next day with all my paperwork in order and was administered a number of tests to determine my aptitude as a pilot.

Ensign Saunders took my finished materials and said, "Return tomorrow at 1300." In military time, 1300 is one o'clock in the afternoon.

I walked through the recruiting office door the next day at exactly 1300.

"Good afternoon, Mr. Gehweiler," he said. "You scored well on all your tests."

My heart was racing.

"I'm sure you'd make an excellent pilot."

My heart raced even faster.

"But the Navy has a requirement that you graduate from college with at least a B average, and from what I've seen from your records, it doesn't look like that's going to happen."

My heart sank. My mother had wanted me to get a good education. She'd sent me to a private boarding school in order to properly prepare me for college. Her plan worked in part because it got me into the University of North Carolina. But when I got there, I was worn out from two years of boarding school, and I failed to apply myself diligently. I had a little too much fun and didn't study often. I was smart enough to still pass my courses, but I certainly didn't take full advantage of the opportunity. Bad choice? It certainly seemed that way.

The ensign cleared his throat. "However, Mr. Gehweiler, I feel I should inform you that the Marine Corps does not have that grade requirement, and their office is right down the hall."

I thought for a minute. The idea of being a Marine felt exciting. Looking back, somehow, I knew it was meant to be. So down the hall I went, and it was the luckiest walk I ever took, because the Marine Corps was the best thing that ever happened to me. The Corps gave me all the confidence and direction I'd ever need. It instilled within me qualities that I've relied upon throughout my life.

I stood in front of the door with the emblem of the U.S. Marine Corps. The realization that I might have a chance to become a Marine filled me with trepidation, but even more so, with inspiration and pride.

"Yes, this is where I want to be," I whispered to myself. "It's where I'm meant to be."

I walked inside. The room was the same size and held the same furniture in the same configuration as the Navy office. But this time, behind the front desk sat a gunnery sergeant in his dress blues. There's not a better-looking uniform in the world than a set of Marine dress blues. He had three rows of ribbons on his chest. I recognized one as a Purple Heart. His name tag read *Savage*, which seemed appropriate given his scowl and tanned head with the standard "high and tight" haircut. A scar ran down the side of his face from ear to chin. The same picture of President Johnson sat behind him, bracketed this time by the U.S. flag and the beautiful red-and-gold flag of the Marine Corps. A corporal sat at the adjacent desk. He had cold black eyes, the same haircut, two rows of ribbons, and ears that stuck out like ping-pong paddles.

"Good morning," the gunnery sergeant said. "What can we do for you?"

I offered the same explanation I'd given the Navy recruiter.

"If your uncle is an admiral in the Navy, why aren't you applying to them?"

"Well, sir, apparently the Navy has a requirement that to be an officer and a pilot, I have to graduate from college with a B average, and ... well, that isn't going to happen. It's my understanding that the Marine Corps doesn't have that requirement."

He stared silently.

I grew nervous.

"First of all, I am a gunnery sergeant in the United States Marine Corps, and not an officer. So you will address me as *Gunnery Sergeant*, not *sir*. It will do you well to remember that distinction going forward should you have a future in the Corps. Second of all, it would appear as though we are your second choice, not your first, which makes me question your depth of commitment."

"Yes, Gunnery Sergeant." I tried to keep my voice from betraying my intense nervousness. "After thinking about it, I am very excited and very hopeful to have an opportunity to be a Marine. Everyone knows they're the most fearsome and respected arm of the service." I hoped I was selling myself. It was the last chance I had to join and fly.

The gunnery sergeant stood and pointed to the small conference table. "Have a seat."

One week later, I took the same flight school tests for the Marine

Corps and again passed with good grades. Two days afterward, I was standing in the Marine Corps recruiting office with six other men as we raised our hands and were inducted. I remember feeling nervous about what lay ahead, but still it was one of the proudest moments of my life.

What lay immediately ahead was sixteen weeks of waiting. I was ordered to report to Officer Candidates School in Quantico, Virginia, but not for four months. I couldn't report earlier due to the influx of candidates supporting the buildup of the Vietnam War.

After graduation from UNC, I returned home to spend time with my mom and work in my grandfather's ferroalloy plant in Niagara Falls, New York. My mother and I lived in nearby Youngstown, a mile down the road from my grandfather.

Patriarch to an impressive family of four daughters and one son, with attending grandchildren, my grandfather was a big, tough Irishman. He'd made a fortune in the coal business in Pittsburgh, just to lose it all during the Great Depression. He was undeterred, however, and over the next several decades, he built, owned, and operated no less than four steel mills, the first of them in Niagara Falls.

He cast a long shadow, and we were all deferential in his presence. He cared for his family, to be sure, but it was on his terms, and it wasn't a good idea to get on his bad side. He liked cigars, brandy, women, his reputation for success, and being recognized by society.

Every summer, he staged a week-long command performance at his estate in Youngstown. Each family member was required to attend, without exception. It was always a great affair and wonderful to have the entire family of thirty or so together at once. But he was in charge, and when he walked into the room the hair on the back of my neck stood up. Everyone would grow slightly on edge. One never knew what kind of a mood he might be in. He had no qualms about delivering a sharp rebuke to one of his adult children in front of everyone if he felt the need. It was "yes, sir," and "no, sir," and walk softly.

A week before I was to report to the mill, he summoned my mother and me for a visit.

"Hey, Mom," I asked, "why do you think he wants us to come over to the house?" It was an unusual invitation for just the two of us.

"Don't worry, honey. He knows you're going into the Marine Corps and probably wants to wish you well."

Wish me well? I thought. *Really?* It didn't seem his style.

The housekeeper let us in and ushered us upstairs to the veranda off my grandfather's master bedroom. The view overlooked the Niagara River and the manicured grounds below. My grandfather was seated at his desk and turned and waved when he saw us. It was rare that he addressed any of his grandchildren other than to say hello and pat them on the head. But he was smiling then.

"Hi, Peg," he said to my mother. "How are you?"

His children referred to my grandfather by his first two initials: C.F. I always found it odd that none of his children referred to him as "father" or anything like that. I'm sure it was his own doing—his egocentric need to enforce his dominance over his children. His grandchildren referred to him as Daddy Colbert, a moniker he chose to perhaps evidence his status as the supreme head of the clan.

"I'm fine, C.F.," my mother said.

Looking directly at me, he smiled. "How about you, son? How are you?"

"I'm fine, Daddy Colbert." I wanted to keep it short and sweet. "Thank you, sir."

"I understand you'll be working at the mill while you're waiting to go into the service."

He said nothing about the Marine Corps, which I'd expected. He never handed out compliments, only observations, and, more frequently, criticisms. Just look at his son, my uncle Dick, who'd opted to attend the Naval Academy rather than join the family business. For this, he was always roundly and rudely criticized, even though he became a famous and well-respected four-star admiral. He served as president of the U.S. Naval War College, was on the short list for chief of naval operations, and his final post was commander in chief of NATO for southern Europe. My grandfather was about business and had little regard for the military and politics.

I stood a little straighter. "Yes, sir."

"Well, make sure you stand tall and do your job." The tone of his voice was rising. "You represent the family, and I expect you to represent it well."

"Yes, sir," I repeated. It sounded as though my voice were coming down a long hallway. He still said nothing about the Marine Corps, nor Vietnam. Not even "Good luck." *You are one hard SOB*, I thought. *That's probably why you're so successful.*

He turned back toward my mother, made a little chitchat, and we were done. Interview over. I knew then that I'd have to stand tall and hold my own in his mill. Little did I realize how much those four months would help prepare me for what I'd encounter at Quantico and beyond.

The mill was nothing like those today. Four huge furnaces dominated the open, two-block-long metal building. The furnaces were made of steel, with brick-lined bowls in the ground. The bowls were filled with materials that would be melted by enormous carbon electrodes, leaving what resembled a huge pile of coal. Charged by powerful electrical cables, these electrodes melted the material from the bottom up.

There was a large shaft, maybe forty feet by forty feet, that ran down from floor level to the bottom of each furnace. Every few hours, a team of two men would descend the shaft to tap the furnace. It was dangerous and terribly hot work. They'd stand on a platform across from the taphole and place a long metal rod on the metal railing with one end on the asphalt "cork" in the taphole. As one man held the rod in place, the other used a sledgehammer to pound on the rod until the cork broke. When that happened, the molten steel in the bottom of the furnace would shoot out in a fiery arc, falling away just before them. It would collect in a large crucible below the taphole. The heat in that shaft at that moment was indescribable.

Once the crucible was full, the team would place a new asphalt cork in the taphole, stemming the flow of steel. An overhead crane that ran on rails along the ceiling of the building would lift the crucible out of the shaft and move it forward to pour it into a large mold. Again, the heat during this pouring process was unimaginable.

The smoke and particulates in the air within the building made it impossible to see more than a few hundred feet. Looking down the floor, the glow from the four furnaces pulsating through the black smoke and dust seemed like what Hades must look like.

The steelworkers faced horrendous working conditions. There were virtually no environmental or safety guidelines, nor protections. These were tough, hard men of Polish, Italian, Hungarian, and a variety of Eastern European backgrounds. Some of them didn't speak much, if any, English.

• • •

On one cold morning in the fall, I showed up in the steel mill clock house at seven o'clock with perhaps fifty other men waiting to put my card into the time clock. Dressed in hard hats and protective work clothes already dirty with wear, they clutched their lunch pails in the dim light emanating from the single bulb swinging from the ceiling.

Each of the men of the morning crew stared at me like I was from Mars. Their single thought was clear: *Who the hell is this?*

They didn't have to wonder long.

The man running the time clock office yelled, "You must be Colbert's grandson, aren't you?"

Every man there knew damn well that Charles F. Colbert owned the mill, and now they knew who I was.

Oh, that's just great, I thought. I meekly nodded.

"You wait until everyone else has checked in," the man barked. "Then I'll get the yard boss."

As each man walked up to check in, he gave me the once-over. Some shook their heads in disdain.

Well, this ought to be fun, I thought.

At last, the yard boss appeared. "Follow me," he growled.

We walked to a corner of the property marked by multiple piles of what looked like big slabs of broken concrete. In reality, they were piles of ferroalloys. After the molds filled with molten steel alloy had cooled, they were picked up by the overhead crane and dropped into these huge Euclid trucks, which then dumped them into piles in the processing yard. Next to these piles were wooden boxes about four feet by four feet wide and three feet tall. Some of them were filled with pieces of ferroalloy.

The foreman handed me a sledgehammer. "Your job," he growled, "is to use this hammer to break off a piece of this material about the size of a basketball and put it in the crate. When you fill one, you can start on the next."

As he walked away, I looked at a long row of boxes in front of me. Clearly, the intention was to make my job as tough as possible to see if I'd quit.

I spent an entire month breaking up the slabs, and no one ever said a word to me, even at lunchtime. Every morning I clocked in, and every morning I grabbed my sledgehammer and headed to the rock piles. I knew everyone was waiting for me to quit, or just not show up one day. But there was no way in hell I was going to quit. I was determined to show them the strength of my will. Plus, the shame of the owner's grandson quitting wasn't something I could even imagine.

One day in the lunchroom, the yard boss, a big Irishman named

2. *The Beginning*

Jack Kelly, called out, "Hey, kid, that hair of yours is kinda long. I think I need to trim it a bit with these shears."

I'd already had enough of that asshole, so I stood up slowly and said, "No, you won't." I'd gained at least a modicum of confidence on the rock piles.

The lunchroom was full, and there was total silence as everyone waited to see what would happen. Kelly was a lot bigger than I was, but I doubted he was willing to get into a physical confrontation with the owner's grandson.

"Jack," one of the men called, "leave the kid alone."

"What's it to you, Polansky?" the foreman bellowed.

Richie Polansky was small of stature but had made something of a name for himself earlier in life as a welterweight boxer. He had the face to prove it, especially his nose. "Well," Richie said, slowly walking my way, "I just think you should leave the kid alone."

"What are you, his fucking nursemaid?"

"No, but the kid's carried his weight so far, so I think you need to just let it go."

I certainly felt I'd carried my weight and was glad to know that someone else agreed. I stood there, frozen in place.

"Okay, Polansky," Kelly barked. "If you think he's so fucking worthy, he starts on your crew tomorrow. We'll see how he handles the furnaces. But for now, he can get his ass back to the rock piles." Kelly turned on his heel and walked out of the lunchroom.

Polansky gave me a wink and turned away. I heard a few mutterings and chuckles, along with the sound of chairs scraping back from tables as the rest of the men in the lunchroom returned to work.

Polansky walked up to me as we all checked out of work that afternoon. "Come with me." He led me across the street to a bar called O'Malley's, where many of the day crew were also gathering.

Well, hell, I thought, *at least it's an Irish bar.* I wondered what my Irish grandfather would think.

Polansky led me inside, and I noticed all the heads turning around toward me. He managed to secure two stools at the bar and motioned for me to sit.

"You're old enough to drink, aren't you?"

"Yes, sir, I am." Hell, in New York state in those days, the drinking age was eighteen, but if you were tall enough to put money on the bar, you could usually get served.

29

"My name ain't *sir*, son. It's Richie. You can save that sir shit for where you're going. I know you're waiting to go into the Marines, and Vietnam shortly afterward. You ever had a boilermaker?"

"No, Richie, can't say I have."

Richie held up two fingers to the bartender, who poured us two mugs of beer and two shots of whiskey. Richie dumped one shot in his beer and the other in mine. He lifted his mug and motioned for me to do the same. He gave me a nod and banged his down in one go.

I made it almost halfway through mine before I had to gasp for air. I could hear more than a few laughs from the crowd.

"That's okay, kid," Richie said, laughing too. "You'll get better with practice."

Perhaps, I thought, but I was more worried about getting home, especially as Richie ordered another round.

My hangover the next day was made even worse by the intense heat of working with Richie's furnace crew. We all wore at least three layers of clothing to protect us from the intense heat emanating from the furnaces. Our job was to keep the floor around the open furnaces clean of debris, which would continually pop out onto the floor as the material cooked inside. Another responsibility was to scrape the slag from the molds as the molten alloy cooled. The molds were about ten by ten feet wide by ten inches deep. We used long-handled rakes to skim off the slag onto the floor and clean that after the cooled molds were dumped into the huge Euclid trucks.

I wore a set of long johns, covered by sweatpants and a hooded sweatshirt, then topped by my heavy work pants and jacket. On top of all of that was a long asbestos coat, heavy gloves, and a helmet with a plastic faceplate. I'd sweat through all of it within minutes around the furnaces. It was difficult work, but much more interesting and exciting than the rock piles.

Richie took me under his wing. "Look, kid, from now on you won't be working by yourself on the rock piles. You'll be with my crew. We're a team, and we depend on one another. I expect you to do everything I tell you, and to be member of this team. You're going to have to hold up your end of the workload. Understand?"

"Yes, sir." I was excited about the opportunity to be part of his team, and one of the men.

"As I said before, I ain't no *sir*. My name's Richie. Got it?" His voice rose a bit.

2. The Beginning

"Yeah, Richie. I got it."

Richie was about five foot six and a lean 160 pounds. His parents had emigrated from Poland after World War II with their three children, escaping the devastation of their country and looking, like so many others, for a chance at a new life. They settled in Niagara Falls, New York, along with many other families from all over Eastern Europe also fleeing the post-war conditions for the hope of America. Niagara Falls, with its thriving industries, was a magnet for many of these men, and the city became rich in ethnic diversity.

On one of our numerous trips to O'Malley's, I asked Richie about his boxing career and how he got started.

"Well, kid, when you grow up short in stature with a short fuse to boot, you learn how to use your fists. I got pretty good on the streets and ended up in a gym not too far from here. I was lucky enough to have a good trainer and eventually got some amateur fights."

I hunched over my boilermaker and stared at his chiseled face. He had scars over both eyes, a terrible-looking ear, and a nose so broken I could only imagine the beatings he'd taken.

"Eventually, I got a few professional fights. The extra money was a big help to the family. I did pretty good for a few years, and almost made it to the welterweight championship fight. A month before the scheduled bout, I had a preliminary match. I got knocked out and had a bad concussion. The boxing commission decided I was done."

I sat silently as Richie looked off into the distance. I could tell he was miles and years away from where we were now.

After a long moment, he turned and smiled at me. "I had my shot," he said. "Make sure you make the best of yours, okay?"

"Yeah, Richie, I will." I signaled for two more boilermakers.

Over the next three months, I gained an enormous amount of respect for Richie and the hard men who worked in the mill. I knew I was only going to be there for four months. Their destiny was to spend their entire working lives in those terrible conditions. Lives that certainly would be cut short by lung disease, cancer, emphysema, and accidents. There were no workers' rights in those days, and those men suffered as a result.

After two months, Richie and his crew moved to the night rotation. I came to really enjoy that shift. All we had to do was keep the furnaces tended and the floors clean of debris. The furnaces weren't tapped, nor molds poured, at night. That meant there was only a skeleton crew, without all the daytime activity or a foreman to make everyone miserable.

The icing on the cake was that every night, the crew brought in food from home. During the day shift, everyone took their lunchboxes to the dining room for their thirty-minute break, but at night, each man brought in dishes prepared by his wife. We ate every kind of Polish, Italian, Hungarian, and Eastern European food you can imagine. They heated it in pans and Dutch ovens atop the molds still warm from the day. That was some of the best food I've ever eaten.

Around 2:00 a.m., we'd take our break and sit around a picnic table near one of the furnaces. Large sections of the side of the building were open to the outside due to intermittent furnace explosions. It was winter in Niagara Falls, so that made for some frigid conditions unless you were near the furnaces. But the food made up for it. There was Polish kielbasa and sauerkraut stuffed in fresh hoagie rolls, steaming bowls of Hungarian goulash, plates of chicken cacciatore and pasta, and maybe some baklava for dessert. We ate like kings, celebrating the rich heritages of the men and the skills of their wives.

I look back on those days at the mill with a lot of fondness for the men I met and the time we shared. We worked hard, and we were a team. It was a testing ground, and it certainly prepared me for what was to come at Quantico and Officer Candidates School.

During those four months, my mother kept me well fed and tended to my occasional aches and pains. My favorite meal was her delicious chili, which I requested often and still cook for myself today.

We lived in a three-story century-old wood-frame house perched on a cliff overlooking Niagara River Gorge. From the back porch, we could see Canada across the river, just before the point where it emptied into Lake Ontario. It was a striking setting.

After I returned home each evening, my mother and I ate dinner together and talked about my day at the mill and my upcoming entrance into the Marine Corps.

"How was your day, Ricky?" she'd always ask.

I told her how tough it was on the rock piles, and how no one would talk to me.

"You know they're testing you, honey," she said. "Just hang in there. You're strong, and I know things will change for the better soon."

Her advice was always correct, and her confidence and support were great.

2. The Beginning

After dinner each night, I hauled myself up the three stories to my room in the attic. There was a dresser in my room with little brass-hinged handles that swung in a rhythmic cadence when the strong winter winds barreled across Lake Ontario and buffeted the old house. The sound helped put me to sleep, although as tired as I usually was, I needed little help.

During the weekends, I'd relax with Mom and our Airedale terrier, Max, on the back porch. I stared over Niagara Gorge into the emerald-green forest of Canada as seagulls wheeled and screeched in the stiff breezes coming off Lake Ontario. It was a good time in my life, and I felt at peace as my departure date approached.

"You know how proud I am of you joining the Marine Corps, don't you, honey?" my mother asked one afternoon.

"Sure, Mom, I know."

"As proud as I am, I'm also worried. Vietnam is getting serious, and I can't bear thinking that something might happen to you." Tears welled in her eyes.

"I'll be fine, Mom. If I can survive the mill and boilermakers with Richie, I can survive anything."

I watched a smile cross her lips.

A week later, Mom and I were at home on Saturday eating lunch in the living room. It was cold outside. A winter storm had come in that morning.

"How's your lunch, honey?"

I glanced down at my bowl of chili. Before I could answer, I heard her gasp. I looked up to see Mom fall from her chair. I rushed over. Her eyes were open, staring at the ceiling. She wasn't breathing.

I tried mouth-to-mouth resuscitation and CPR for twenty minutes. It seemed like an eternity. There was no result. I called for an ambulance. I knew it would take time for the paramedics to get to our rural area. It didn't matter, though. She had no pulse and was certainly dead. I know now that she was dead the moment she hit the floor.

I put a pillow under her head and closed her eyelids. The wind off the lake increased, ushering in a heavier snowfall. The old house began to creak and groan, almost as though it felt my pain and was registering its own sadness for her passing. I sat on the floor with Mom, watching the swirling snow, and holding her hand. I cried as wonderful memories flooded my brain.

I called my aunt and uncle, who lived in the next town over. They said they'd meet us at the hospital. The ambulance arrived. The medics tried to resuscitate Mom, but I knew it was long over. I climbed into the ambulance, and we headed for the hospital. The driver called in on his radio and reported he was headed in with a DOA. I knew she was gone, but that term drove it home with a vengeance. I was devastated, and never felt more alone in my life.

I spent the next week in a fog, trying to work through all the funeral arrangements and legal issues. Relatives and friends came and went, offering their condolences.

My uncle told me that my father, who had disappeared when I was two, had contacted him and was coming to the funeral. He asked if I'd pick him up at the airport. Me? Really? I'd had no contact with him for more than twenty years and felt no desire to change that. Nonetheless, I got roped into airport duties. My uncle gave me a photo to help identify him.

As he walked off the plane, all I could think was, *Who the hell is this?*

He was short and fat, wearing a sports jacket and a porkpie hat with a short feather in it. He looked like the cover model for a magazine for used car salesmen. I learned much later in life that was indeed one of the many jobs he'd held.

I was a very fit six-foot, 150-pound, blond-haired, blue-eyed young man who was wondering how he'd gotten switched at birth.

It was a long ride back to my aunt and uncle's house, where I was staying. All my father did was talk about how unfair and difficult his life had been. "I'm sorry about your mother, son, and I'm sorry that I wasn't a bigger part of your life. Life hasn't been easy for me. Can't ever seem to find a job that I like, and of course there are the problems with my wife's family, who are not well. But I do have an opportunity to manage a hardware store, and I hope that will be the job I can stay with."

"Yeah, well, right now I'm concentrating on getting through the funeral arrangements and legal details." I left it at that.

I couldn't get over how different we were, and how little we had in common.

An hour later, we arrived at my aunt and uncle's house. We spent the next hour listening to more details of how difficult his life had been. For God's sake, my mother had just died, and all he could do was talk about his own problems. By the end of the next two days, it was all I could do not to strangle that whimpering and weak excuse for a man.

34

2. The Beginning

I guess I should have thanked him for leaving when I was a toddler. Bottom line, it was a blessing and not a loss that he was never in my life. I can't imagine what life would have been like with him around, and what an anchor he would have been. After Mom's funeral, I paid for a cab to take him to the airport. Surprisingly, it wasn't the last time I heard from him. He contacted me years later to ask if I could lend him money. He died of alcoholism a few years afterward.

By the time I was to report to Quantico, I was more than ready to get the hell out of there. I was truly on my own then, and in some strange way, it was exhilarating. I was about to walk through a door into another dimension. What lay beyond that door, and what did the future hold for me? I was sure of only one thing: it would change my life forever.

Officer Candidates School is basically boot camp for officers-to-be, and I hoped it would prove to be my salvation. Would it force me to focus on what was at hand, and not dwell on my mother's death? Would it give me what I'd subconsciously craved—direction, structure, purpose, and confidence? Would I be strong and determined enough to master the training and challenges? I was about to find out.

3

Quantico

Seven days after my mother's death, I arrived at Quantico, ready to enter the Marine Corps Officer Candidates School. I was among forty young men from all over the country with every type of background.

We all boarded a yellow school bus at five o'clock on a dark, cold, rainy January morning just outside the gates to the base. The bus was unlighted inside. There were a few murmurs as we boarded.

"No talking!" the bus driver loudly rebuked us.

We all sat silently in the dark, each with his own thoughts about what lay ahead. You could cut the tension with a knife.

I'd thought about that moment for a long time. I knew I was going to be tested beyond anything I could imagine. But I'd told myself for months that tens of thousands of young men had passed this way, and by God, if they could do it, then I sure as hell could. I had an immense sense of pride knowing that when I came through the process, I'd be an officer in the U.S. Marine Corps, and there was nothing more prideful or respected than that.

As the bus passed through the arch of the base entrance on that pitch-black morning, the rain increased, illuminated by the head-lights. Falling silver needles pierced the dark as they exploded onto the water-covered asphalt ahead. We were entering another world.

A few minutes later, we pulled up in front of the processing build-ing, hidden behind a row of glaring floodlights aimed at the bus. We sat silently in the dark bus for what seemed like an eternity.

At last, the interior lights burst on. A short, stocky drill sergeant stood at the front of the bus. His starched uniform fit so tightly, it looked sprayed on. The two rows of ribbons pinned above his left shirt pocket attested to his stature in the Corps. His classic DI hat shadowed his face. There was dead silence as he stood staring at us.

"My name is Sergeant Jordan." His bark was like a bullhorn. "You will address me as Sergeant. Any time you are addressed by me or any other sergeant here at Quantico, you will reply, 'Yes, Sergeant.' Do you understand?"

Everyone on the bus loudly replied, "Yes, Sergeant!"

"WHAT THE FUCK WAS THAT?" Sergeant Jordan screamed. "I CAN'T HEAR YOU!"

"YES, SERGEANT!" we replied even more loudly.

His booming voice continued. "When you exit my bus, you will put your sorry-ass feet on the yellow footprints outside. Do you understand?"

"YES, SERGEANT!" we screamed as loudly as we could.

His voice rose even higher when he barked again, "Now get the fuck off my bus! NOW! NOW! NOW!"

Forty bodies scrambled from their seats, rushed down the aisle, and tumbled out the door.

"GO! GO! GO! MOVE! MOVE! MOVE!" the DI screamed.

The purpose was, of course, to deliver as much shock as possible the moment the recruits entered boot camp. The mission of boot camp is to peel away every layer of the civilian world the candidate has known, and to rebuild that man into a Marine.

It's a crucial undertaking that requires as much mental and physical pressure as possible to ensure the graduate can perform under extreme conditions. These men were destined to be officers and would be responsible for leading other Marines into combat. Succumbing to the pressure of combat isn't an option when men's lives are on the line. Boot camp is designed both to train these men and eliminate the individuals incapable of meeting the standards required of a Marine Corps officer.

My time on the rock piles would come in handy. I was going to keep my head down, my mouth shut, and my eyes on the goal line.

Once out of the bus, we all stood in formation, our feet planted on the yellow footprints on the pavement in front of the processing building. We stared into the brilliant floodlights that obscured the building behind them.

"Get your sorry asses at attention," Sergeant Jordan bellowed. "You will go through the double doors in front of you when I tell you. You will go in in groups of five. Do you understand?"

"YES, SERGEANT!"

The sergeant raised his voice even higher. "WHAT THE FUCK

WAS THAT? Are you idiots already tired? Is it too early for you? Do you wish you were home with your mommy?" At a crescendo, he bellowed, "WELL, I'M YOUR FUCKING MOMMY NOW! DO YOU UNDERSTAND?"

We screamed as loud as we could: "YES, SERGEANT!"

Standing in front of the formation, he barked and pointed. "You first five move your asses through that door. MOVE!"

The first five men ran forward and entered the building. The rest of us stood at attention, waiting to see what would happen. Only a few minutes later, the five guys returned with their heads shaved to a barely discernable stubble. They planted themselves back in formation.

"You next five get your asses in there," the sergeant boomed.

So it went. I was in the third of the four rows. It was bitterly cold, and I saw guys shivering. Each group was in and out in minutes, heads shaved to the skin. Some were bleeding from warts or bumps that had fallen prey to the electric razors.

The freezing rain formed little balls of ice crystals on the stubble of the men in front of me. The light from the floodlights lit up the crystals. All I could think was, *Geez, each head kinda looks like a light bulb. Or maybe a tiara. Sure as hell glad Sergeant Jordan can't hear what I'm thinking. Fairly sure the tiara thing wouldn't go well.*

My turn came, and I ran through the door with four others. There were five barber chairs, each with a barber behind it. The floor was covered in mounds of hair.

The first barber was a big black man with a southern accent. He shouted, "Sit yo asses in these chairs," and we did.

Each barber made four or five passes with an electric razor, taking all remnants of hair with it. Maybe two minutes later, we were back out the door and in formation. Forty bald, cold, shell-shocked young men stood in the dark and freezing rain waiting for whatever would happen next. Shaving all our hair was another way of removing part of our identity. The peeling of the onion had begun.

For two days, we were marched from classroom to barracks to classroom and back during the orientation process. We were still in our civilian clothing. The idea was to humiliate us by implying, "You're not even good enough to wear Marine fatigues yet."

On the second day, we marched to breakfast, a standard cafeteria setup in the mess hall. We were all hungry all the time. I piled my metal tray high with everything. The food was pretty good, except for the pancakes, which tasted like cardboard. When I finished everything else, I took my tray to the end of the line where the dirty trays were stacked.

A big sergeant bellowed at me, "What the fuck do you think you're doing?"

"Putting my tray away, Sergeant," I said meekly.

"You see the stripes on my sleeve, you idiot? Those are the stripes of a staff sergeant. You will address me and any other Marine wearing those stripes as *staff sergeant*. Do you understand me?"

"Yes, Staff Sergeant, sir," I replied. Error.

"*Sir?*" he screamed. "Do you see any fucking officer's bars on my shoulder, you idiot? I am a staff sergeant in the United States Marine Corps. Don't ever refer to me or any other noncommissioned officer as *sir* ever! Do you understand?" By the time he finished yelling, his face was red, and he had spittle on his lips.

I had this horrible feeling I was about to laugh. That would be bad. "Yes, Staff Sergeant!" I screamed.

He stared down at the pancakes on my tray. "You take that fucking tray back to that table and don't bring that goddamn thing back here until it's empty." The word *fuck* was popular in the Corps in those days. "We don't waste anything in the Marine Corps. Do you understand?"

"Yes, Staff Sergeant!"

I returned to my table and could feel him still staring at me. I took a bite. The pancake seemed to expand in my mouth. When the staff sergeant finally looked away, no doubt distracted by some other miscreant, I grabbed a napkin in each hand and scooped up the rest of the syrup-laden pancakes and stuffed them into my overcoat pockets. I marched back up to the line and deposited my tray with the others. I made brief eye contact with the sergeant as he glowered at me again. I briefly considered mentioning how good the pancakes were but thought better of it.

The following day, we were issued fatigues, and put our civilian clothes into storage. Two years later, I had occasion to wear that overcoat again. I remember putting my hands into the pockets and thinking: *What the hell is all this stuff in here?* I remembered back to that morning and had a good laugh. That's referred to as a good flashback.

We'd been assigned to specific squad bays in the two-story barracks. Each level had a long room with windows lining each wall. Between each window was a bunk bed. At the end of the beds were two footlockers that stood side by side. At the other end of the room was the common shower and bathroom facility. This was to be our home for twelve weeks.

Creating chaos is the best way to test a man's ability to cope—and the drill instructors at Quantico were experts at it. The squad bay was the perfect environment for them to unleash all manner of chaos. Daily, we'd be treated to four drill sergeants screaming and unleashing commands that were impossible to complete. They'd overturn bunks not properly made and empty foot lockers on the floor for no reason. Forty recruits had to scramble around and try to get their shit together.

We spent those twelve weeks under constant pressure. We performed nearly endless physical training, endured repeated trips through the obstacle course, marched in formation, marched through the terrain, and competed in pugil stick matches. We also spent time in class to learn about the history of the Marine Corps, along with a variety of leadership skills. Staying awake in class was a challenge. We were exhausted.

My favorite part of training was marching in formation. The rasping bark of the DI and his mesmerizing cadence moving the whole platoon as one was almost intoxicating. Each DI had his own special voice and cadence routine. They were good at this and took enormous pride in how well they could march a platoon.

Once we were proficient at marching and responding to commands as a unit, some of us had the chance to march the platoon. I loved it. I developed a pretty good bark and style. I'd have done that every day if given the opportunity.

Those who survived the twelve weeks of training were different men afterward. We would be different for the rest of our lives. The wash-out rate was about 40 percent. Officers-to-be had to be tougher and more determined than the men they were to lead—the training at Quantico was designed to make them just that.

Two weeks before graduation, one of the squad bay sergeants asked us to fill out a form identifying any dignitaries in our family who might attend the graduation ceremony. My uncle, Richard "Dick" Colbert, who'd inspired me to join the service, was then a three-star vice admiral attached to the State Department in nearby Washington, D.C.

Later that afternoon, a sergeant stormed into the squad bay. "Gehweiler!" he screamed. "Get your ass up here! What the hell is this? Your uncle is a three-star admiral? You better not be fucking around here,

Gehweiler, because it just so happens our commanding officer is a two-star general and will be outranked."

"Sorry, Sergeant." I shrugged slightly. "But that's what he is."

The sergeant stormed out as the guys in the squad smiled and each gave me a silent thumbs-up. Oh yeah. One for the peons.

Graduation day finally came, and with it a tremendous sense of pride and accomplishment. I'd made it. I was an officer in the United States Marine Corps. As per tradition, one of our platoon drill sergeants pinned on my second lieutenant bars and saluted me. I returned his salute and, as per tradition, gave him a dollar bill.

My dear uncle was standing there, watching me receive my bars. I could tell he was proud. I turned and gave him what was, of course, to me the most important salute I'd ever give. He returned it, and we shared a big bear hug.

Struggling with some emotion, I managed to say, "Uncle Dick, I can't tell you how much it means to me for you to be here."

"Rick, I wouldn't have missed it for the world. The whole family is proud of you, and I know your mother is watching and feels very proud too. Well done, Lieutenant."

OCS Quantico, A Company, 1st Platoon, April 1967. I'm in the fourth row from the bottom, third from the left (author's collection).

"Thank you, Admiral." I smiled.

Training had been long and difficult, but I'd made it, and I was going to give myself a graduation present. There was a Chevrolet dealership in town, and in its window was a beautiful 1967 Corvette convertible. It was British racing green with tan leather interior. It had a 350/327 engine with a 4/11 rear end. Bottom line, it was a badass set of wheels that could hop off the line like a rocket ship.

I'd made a down payment weeks earlier, and I walked in that afternoon and signed the final papers. In those days, a new officer, especially one who was going to become an aviator, could buy almost anything with just a signature on the loan papers. The seller knew he could always collect from Uncle Sam should anything happen.

In addition to Uncle Dick, my aunt Dot had come down for the graduation from Pittsburgh. I was to drive her back home and spend a few days with her before heading off to Pensacola. I showed up in my new car.

"Are we driving back to Pittsburgh in that?" Her eyes were as big as saucers.

"You bet we are, Aunt Dot. And we're gonna have a ball. You'll be the talk of the neighborhood when we get there."

"*If* we get there, young man," she said, her voice trembling. "You make sure we do."

"I promise to keep it under eighty," I said with a smile.

The five-hour drive took us four.

Three days later, I hopped into my dream car and headed south to Pensacola, Florida, and naval flight school, where I'd learn to become a naval aviator. Marine aviators went through the naval flight program because the fact is that the Marine Corps is a department of the Navy. The Navy boys were always quick to point that out.

"As a matter of fact, it is," we were fond of replying with big, snarky smiles. "It's called the men's department."

4

Pensacola

The drive to Pensacola was fantastic. After all those weeks of pressure and confinement at Quantico, driving that Corvette with the top down all by myself, I felt on top of the world. I thought that when I got there, I'd have to beat the girls off with a stick. A good-looking brand-new Marine lieutenant in a brand-new Corvette. How could they resist?

Driving into Pensacola was a blast of reality. Christ, every freaking Navy ensign, and Marine lieutenant was driving a Corvette, a Jaguar, or a Mustang. Mr. Cool was just one more cow in the herd.

I still loved my Corvette. The convertible top had two release handles on the top of the windshield that were easily reachable from the driver's seat. I could unfasten the latches and flip back the whole top into the rear storage deck in one quick movement, without ever leaving my seat.

It was especially impressive when a couple of gals pulled up next to you at a stop light. One, two, three, and a big smile as I began the maneuver. It did pay off from time to time.

There was a big backup of officers waiting to enter the flight program in those days. The program graduated a group of about forty every week, but the influx of officers was greater than that. As a result, we were on hold. Well, not exactly on hold.

Each morning, the pool of officers would report for PT (physical training). We'd just finished twelve weeks of PT at Quantico and were in pretty damn good shape. Or so we thought. The PT was run by Marine drill instructors who loved making it as difficult as they could now that we were officers. After several hours of drills, we ended the morning festivities with a run through the obstacle course. Hell, we'd run the obstacle course at Quantico more times than we could count. The difference was that this obstacle course was at the beach ... in the sand. I don't know how many times I ran it at Pensacola, but I know I puked every time.

The rest of the day, we were on our own. We had the option to live at the BOQ (Bachelor Officers' Quarters) for free if we wanted. But almost all of us elected to rent houses in town or at the beach. The pool time lasted almost two months. It was like a spring break fraternity party every day and night. In those days, gals from all over the country found their way to Pensacola in search of a handsome Marine or Navy officer. The officers' club in Pensacola on a Friday night was something to behold. The parties at our beach houses seemed to never end.

I shared a house with two Marines—Rick Graham and Butch Korosec. (Yup, that's his real name.) We had a ball. One afternoon sitting around the dining room table, Butch mentioned there was going to be a swim meet at the base pool and he was going to enter.

"What are you talking about?" Graham asked.

"There's a competition swim meet next week at the base pool. There's going to be a lot of college swim teams, but it's an open competition and I'm going to enter."

"Are you nuts?" Graham replied. "Those will be some of the best swimmers in the country."

"Yeah, I know," Butch said with a shrug. "But I'm going to give it a try anyway."

"You're going to get your ass smoked," I said. "What event are you going to enter?"

"I don't know." Butch shrugged again. "Why don't you guys pick?"

Graham and I looked at one another, shook our heads, and smiled. Knowing it was the most difficult event offered, Graham suggested, "How about the butterfly?"

"Okay. Sure. I guess," Butch responded.

The following week, Rick and I headed to the base pool house to watch the competition. The pool house contained an eight-lane Olympic-size pool. We walked toward the stadium seats on the right side of the room. The interior was bathed in brilliant light from the numerous overhead banks of lights. The air hung heavy with humidity and the smell of chlorine. The black lane lines on the bottom of the pool shimmered through the aquamarine water as competitors began taking warmup laps, cutting sharp wakes through the smooth surface of the water. After half an hour, the different events began. Soon it was time for the butterfly.

There was Butch in his Speedos with a Marine emblem on the side, perched on the stand in the middle lane. Rick and I looked at one another.

"Man, this could be really embarrassing," I whispered. "I'm almost afraid to watch. Almost."

A voice over the loudspeaker rang out. "Swimmers, take your positions."

Butch stepped forward and bent over, his toes curled around the edge of the starting platform. He actually looked like he knew what he was doing.

The loudspeaker crackled again. "Swimmers, on your marks, get set..." The gun went off. Eight swimmers rocketed off their platforms in unison and knifed into the water.

Four lengths of the pool. Butch was in third place, about one length behind, at the second turn. He began to close the gap halfway down the third lap. Then Butch was tied for the lead at the last turn. We were standing and screaming as he pulled away in the home stretch. He beat the guy in second by a full length. We were stunned.

"What the fuck was that?" I yelled at Rick as we punched one another in the shoulder and slapped high fives. We looked down at Butch, who was still in the water, draped over the line rope. He looked up at us with a huge grin, then shot us the bird. We bent over with laughter.

Turns out Butch had been All-American in the butterfly at Penn State. What a sneaky bastard. What a great "fuck you!" We got a lot of mileage out of that story over the years.

After two months of PT and parties, we entered the flight program. We began with classes in aerodynamics, engine design, weather, communications, and general aviation protocol. Soon we were flying with instructors, initially in the T-34, learning the basics of how to fly. We practiced takeoffs and landings until our solo day, when the instructor took us out to one of the surrounding airstrips and climbed out of the aircraft.

"Okay, you're ready, Lieutenant. Take off, make a couple of loops around the field, then come back for a landing and pick me up."

I'd done it dozens of times before, but the thrill of your first solo is special, as any pilot will tell you. I took off, and then I was up there all by myself. Blue sky. Big, puffy clouds. What a sense of freedom. I was grinning so widely my face hurt. My smile was still there when I landed and picked up the instructor.

He climbed in and looked over at me. "How does it feel?" he asked through his own grin.

"Unbelievable. Just unbelievable."

Soon afterward, we graduated to the more powerful T-28, which was a great aircraft. It looks kind of like a World War II fighter, with a sliding cockpit cover, front and rear seats, and dual controls.

After another ten months of classes in operating systems, aerodynamics, navigation, communications, and daily flight training, we were all pretty good pilots. We were proficient at aerobatics, flying in close formation, tail-chase engagement, navigation, flying on instruments only, and landing on a dime. We were good—or at least we thought we were.

After a year of intense training in the T-34 and T-28, the Marine pilots were transitioned into whatever aircraft we were going to be assigned to in the real world. In 1968, Vietnam was at full throttle, and maybe one out of every thirty Marine pilots continued into fixed-wing aircraft. The rest of us were destined to become helicopter pilots.

Whatever happened to that image I had of sitting in the cockpit of

T-28 Primary fixed wing trainer, Naval Flight School, Pensacola, Florida (courtesy Jim Berg, USMCR).

4. Pensacola

an A-4, flying close-support combat missions for the grunts in the bush? I wondered.

Our first training helicopter was the Bell H-13, just like the one in the TV series *M*A*S*H*. It had a bubble cockpit for two pilots who sat side by side with dual controls. There were no wheels, just skids. It was kind of a sports car, really.

The first flight day, my instructor took me out to a field maybe five acres in size—a cow pasture for all intents and purposes. He landed and began reviewing the controls systems. He'd already done one tour in Vietnam. He looked at me. "Okay, Lieutenant, I want you to take the stick when I tell you."

The stick is called a cyclic, and it protrudes up from the floor between the pilot's legs. It's how you steer the aircraft. Just like a fixed wing. Kind of.

"The helicopter," he said, "will go anywhere you point the stick. Push forward, it goes forward. Push to the right, it goes to the right. Left is left, and back is back. Got it?"

"Yes, sir." *What's not to get?* I thought.

He put the helicopter into a hover and gave me a quick demonstration. Twenty-foot hover, forward, right, left, and back. Then back to the ground. Smooth as silk.

"You need to use very light pressure on the stick. This isn't a freaking fixed wing that you can jerk around. Got it?"

"Got it."

"Okay, hotshot, I'm going to put us in a hover, and when I tell you, take the stick and repeat what I did."

"Yes, sir."

Up we went. "Okay, take the stick."

I did and tried to gently push on the cyclic. We lurched forward. *Shit!* I thought. Gentle wasn't the word for what I did. Just thinking about moving the stick is enough.

"Goddamn it!" the instructor barked. "I said GENTLY."

No shit, I thought. I got a little better as I went through the other motions, but our movement remained jerky.

After I made a few more rotations, the instructor cleared his throat. "I have the stick," he said.

I let go immediately and he put the Bell H-13 back on the ground.

"On your left is the collective." He pointed. The collective is a lever anchored to the floor at one end and can be raised or lowered like a

47

pump handle. "Raise the collective and the helicopter goes up. Lower the collective and the helicopter goes down. Got it?"

Yup, got it, I thought. "Yes, sir!" I replied.

"Raising the collective increases the pitch on the rotor blades, grabbing more air, which gives us the lift we need to go up. However, as the pitch increases, the RPMs drop off due to the increased load on the engine. Not enough RPMs means you crash. To compensate, you'll need to add power. You do that by turning the rotating throttle handle [just like a motorcycle throttle] at the end of the collective. Keeping the RPMs constant is critical. Not enough RPMs and you crash."

I wish he'd stop saying that.

"When you raise the collective, you need to add power by turning the throttle to the left. Got it?"

I wish he'd stop saying that as well. I nodded.

"Conversely, when we push the collective down, the pitch on the rotor blades decreases, thereby decreasing lift, and we go down. But the RPMs will increase as the load on the engine decreases, so we need to reduce power by rotating the throttle to the right to maintain constant RPMs."

I waited for the "Got it?" part, but he just looked at me. I nodded.

"Okay, so the drill is lift up the collective and add power by turning the throttle to the left. Look at the RPM gauge to coordinate the power with the RPMs. Push the collective down and decrease power by turning the throttle to the right and again coordinating the power with the RPMs to keep them constant. Lift up, power on, push down, power off. Got it?"

Seemed simple enough. Up on, down off. "Got it," I repeated.

He put us into another hover, but this time around fifty feet up. "Okay, I have the rest of the aircraft," he said. "Just work with the collective, and again.... GENTLY! Go ahead."

I pulled slowly up on the collective, keeping my eye on the RPM gauge. As the RPMs began to decrease, I turned the throttle a little. The RPMs shot up. *Shit! Too much throttle.* I backed off a bit. What seemed like it should be simple was anything but. Pushing the collective up and down and trying to keep the RPMs constant was challenging, to say the least. After a while, it became a little easier, but still not exactly smooth.

The instructor took control of the aircraft and set it back down. "Next we're going to work with the rudder pedals," he said. "Push on the right one and the aircraft will rotate to the right. Hold it down and you'll make a three-hundred-and-sixty-degree circle. Push the left one and you'll rotate to the left in the same manner. You can make any part of any turn by coordinating the pressure on the pedals."

I felt the next words coming.

"Got it?"

I could have made a lot of money betting on that response. "Yes, sir," I replied, thinking I might have said "got it" enough. I didn't want to be too much of a smartass, plus he was a captain with a combat tour in Vietnam. He did indeed deserve my respect.

Back into a hover we went.

"Okay, Lieutenant, I have the aircraft. Put your feet on the rudder pedals. Now remember, push *gently*! First, press down on the right rudder pedal."

I complied, and we rotated to the right, a bit more rapidly than either of us would have liked. He glared at me. I tried to smooth it out. We worked both left and right pedals, cutting donuts through the air until I got slightly better.

He put us back on terra firma. "Okay, hotshot," he said. "I want you to take all three controls, put us in a hover, and try to keep the helicopter somewhere within this five-acre field."

I was determined to make this go well. Focus. Focus. *You got this*, I told myself. *Confidence. Focus.*

I placed my right hand on the cyclic, my left hand on the collective and throttle, and my feet on the rudder pedals. Up collective, increase the throttle, keep the cyclic and rudder pedals neutral. We rose slowly and somewhat jerkily into a thirty-foot hover, swaying a bit, then a bit more as I tried to center us with light pressure on the stick.

I got it. I got it, I told myself. Then we veered upward and sideways. *Shit! I ain't got it!*

The instructor grabbed the controls. "I have the aircraft!" he barked.

I released the controls, and he set us back down.

So there I was. I felt humbled. I'd earned my Navy wings. I was a naval aviator, an accomplishment few people can claim. I could land a fixed-wing T-28 in your backyard. I thought I was pretty good. But flying a helicopter was obviously a whole different ball game. I was going to have to learn to fly all over again.

I looked over at the instructor. To my surprise, he wore a huge grin.

"Yeah, I know. I felt the same way on my first day. Trust me, you'll get this, and you'll get good at it. You'll find this more fun and challenging than any fixed-wing."

He was right. I would get good. We all would. We'd be able to do things with a helicopter that are difficult to imagine. But we still had a lot to learn.

Case in point: what to do in the event of an engine failure.

When a fixed-wing aircraft loses an engine, it can still make an emergency landing using its inherent glide slope. Glide slope is the angle and distance a plane can glide before it hits the ground. An aircraft's glide slope is determined by the area of its wings in relation to its overall weight. The larger and longer the wings and the lighter the aircraft, the longer it can stay aloft. That's why gliders can stay in the air for especially long periods of time. Conversely, a short, heavy aircraft with short, stubby wings such as the A-4 jet has a short glide slope, and little ability to make an emergency landing. Ejection is usually the only option when an engine is lost.

None of this pertains to helicopters. They have no wings. Their glide slope is straight down. Without an engine, a helicopter has all the flight characteristics of a safe. There are no ejection options. Pilots don't wear parachutes because egressing from the cockpit as the helicopter falls downward is impossible—there's also the matter of the rotor blades overhead.

There is a maneuver to survive an engine failure, however. It's called autorotation. We practiced it over and over again. Our instructors frequently, and without warning, reached over and turned off the engine. The student then had to immediately drop the collective to the floor to reduce the rotor blades to a flat pitch, minimizing the drag and the loss of RPMs of the rotor head. Then, with firm forward pressure on the cyclic and some rudder coordination to keep the aircraft aligned straight ahead, we'd push the nose of the aircraft over, increasing our airspeed downward in order to increase the airflow over the rotor blades and keep the RPMs up as much as possible.

The move is almost like a child's pinwheel toy. The more you blow on it, the faster it spins. Without the necessary RPMs to keep the rotor blades acting like wings, the helicopter will simply plummet downward. The procedure in that event, as we were fond of saying, is to unstrap, lean over, and kiss your balls goodbye.

Under autorotation, as the aircraft approached around fifty feet off the ground, we'd raise its nose to slow the descent. In smooth coordination, we'd fully pull the collective upward, increasing the pitch of the rotor blades to create just the right amount of lift to land the aircraft safely. The key element is that without the engine to add power, there's only one chance to use the collective to make the transition. Transitioning too high means a rough landing or a crash. Transitioning too late means a rough landing or a crash. If it was all done properly, the H-13 would come to a smooth, sliding landing on its skids in one of the multiple grass training fields surrounding Pensacola.

After the Bell H-13, we transitioned to the bigger and much-heavier Sikorsky H-34, which I'd end up flying in Vietnam. Ungainly in appearance, it was beautiful to the pilots who flew it. It was a workhorse for the Marine helicopter effort throughout the war. It was durable and dependable, if not the strongest of helicopters, especially in the heat and altitude of the northern sectors of the war.

After another month of H-34 training, I completed my time in Pensacola. My next stop was Marine Corps Air Station Santa Ana, in California, for six weeks of training in advanced combat tactics. Then I'd be deployed to South Vietnam.

At Pensacola, we'd been so immersed in classes and flying lessons, we never paid much attention to what waited beyond that. As we headed west for combat training, the reality of where we were going and what we'd be doing began to creep into our collective consciousness.

5

The Edge of the Envelope

We reported to MCAS Santa Ana one week after our Pensacola graduation. We were excited about our new training, and also to be in California. Most of us rented oceanfront apartments in Newport Beach. The college fraternity atmosphere we'd enjoyed in Pensacola continued at full throttle.

In Santa Ana, we flew with instructors who'd all flown the H-34 for at least one tour in Vietnam. We practiced advanced combat tactics mostly designed for getting into and out of hot landing zones. This was critical for the type of flying that would be required of us. We trained hard. We got good. We all hoped it would be good enough. For only some of us, it would.

During our last week of advanced combat tactics, we were practicing what's referred to as max gross weight takeoffs and landings. The aircraft was loaded with iron-filled ammo boxes to simulate a heavy, full load. Then, with our instructors, we'd head out to the mountains around Santa Ana and practice approaches into and out of landing zones that had been carved out of the hillsides at various locations. The elevations and terrain were similar to what we'd find in Vietnam. The LZs were maybe an acre square, cut into the trees on sloped hillsides.

On our last training day, we'd made several approaches and egresses. All had gone well.

My instructor, Captain Dave Stewart, keyed the mic. "Okay, Lieutenant, you're doing well. Let's do one more and head home."

The winds in the Santa Ana Mountains can make for some challenging conditions, especially during approaches and exits from the LZs. They're frequently strong, gusty, and unpredictable. As we approached the last LZ, I struggled with the wind coming from the left. Using a lot of left rudder, additional power, and strong left cyclic, I was able to side slip the 34 into the zone. We settled on what was probably a fifteen- to twenty-degree slope, pointing uphill. It felt like it was about forty-five degrees.

"Okay," Captain Stewart said. "Good job. Let's pick her up and get out of here."

The wind was really picking up, and it buffeted the aircraft as we sat in the zone. I pulled on full power, raised the collective, and sustained a three-foot hover. At that moment, a strong gust of wind hit us from the left, pushing the large nose of the 34 to the right. I was at full power and pushing in the left rudder to realign the nose back to the upslope position, but that caused the RPMs to drop slightly. The rotor head spins to the right. Trying to turn the aircraft to the left against that rotation required more power, and we simply didn't have any more. I couldn't put the aircraft back on the ground either—we were pointing across the slope, which would have risked the 34 rolling over on its side.

As the wind continued to push us toward the trees on the side of the LZ, the captain and I both knew we were in trouble. We still didn't have enough power to realign the aircraft back upslope against the wind, and we were pointing downwind, which caused loss of lift. We began to settle as the tree line approached.

"I have the aircraft!" Captain Stewart yelled.

It all happened in a few seconds. As we continued to spin to the right in an attempt to gain some RPMs, the tail of the 34 touched the trees on the edge of the clearing. The tail rotor of a helicopter is designed to keep the aircraft flying straight. The vertical rotation of the tail blades counterbalances the impulse of the aircraft itself to rotate counter to the main rotor blades. Without the tail rotor, the helicopter will just spin uncontrollably to the right and crash.

That's exactly what we did.

We cut a path one hundred yards down the side of the mountain, taking out trees like a giant lawn mower. Limbs, branches, and debris flew everywhere. Still falling sideways and downward, we slammed into the bottom of the ravine. The rotor blades were thrashing into the ground, throwing dirt, rocks, and splintered wood up into a huge dark cloud. As the blades broke apart, they took out the top of the cockpit, covering the captain and me in more dirt and debris.

Captain Stewart engaged the emergency rotor brake handle above our heads to stop the rotor blades from continuing to break the aircraft apart. As they finally stopped, there was nothing but silence. The captain and I looked at one another, both soaked in fuel and hydraulic fluid and covered in dirt.

The H-34's skin was made of magnesium alloy. If it caught fire, it burned with incredible intensity and rapidity. Any little spark could set it off. We were lying on our left side.

Captain Stewart was strapped into the left seat, which was below me. "Get out now!" he yelled.

In a fog, I unstrapped and climbed up through the cockpit door.

He was pushing me from behind, yelling, "Out! Out!"

Once out of the cockpit, I slid down the side of the helicopter and fell in a heap on the ground below. Captain Stewart did the same. We clambered up the slope to get away from the helicopter in the event it caught fire or exploded.

Also aboard our flight were a crew chief and another Marine who'd come along for the ride, just to log some airtime. It had been an unlucky choice, but a lucky outcome. I bet he's still telling that story over a beer now and then.

The crew chief had been wearing his required safety harness and tether. When the 34 lost its tail rotor in the initial contact with the trees, the helicopter made one violent jerk to the left, causing the crew chief to be ejected through the open door. His safety harness had a long tether to it, which saved his life as it jerked him right back into the aircraft through the same door. He busted a couple of ribs, but it was the only injury sustained in the crash—an absolute miracle. By all rights, we all should have been killed in such a violent crash.

Once we were all out of the aircraft, we sat down and tried to process what had happened. We didn't say much. We were all in shock. I remember feeling a sense of failure and guilt for what happened. To this day, I relive the sequence of events. I accepted long ago that the situation and the conditions dictated the outcome. Still, I felt terrible.

It took several hours before anyone at the base realized we were missing. They eventually sent another helicopter, which transported four shaken Marines back to base. The noise in the belly was so loud we had no way of talking on our way back, so each of us was left with his own thoughts.

The purpose of that training flight had been to test the limits of the aircraft at maximum weight and high altitude—the edge of the flight envelope. Well, we found it for sure.

The bad news was, of course, that we'd crashed. The good news was that we'd all survived, and that experience with the edge of the flight envelope would save my life several times in the coming year.

There was a short debrief and not much else, which surprised me. I never even knew what the accident report said.

The next day, a big H-53 hoisted what was left of the H-34 from the ravine and returned it to the base. The whole squadron walked out to take a look. Everyone stared.

The rotor head was still intact, but only about a foot of each rotor blade remained. The front wheel struts had been torn off, the top of the cockpit was obliterated, and of course, the tail rotor was gone. Not much else but the bulk of the body remained.

How in the hell did we survive? I thought. *How lucky were we that it didn't catch fire? No one would have escaped.*

Several of my pilot buddies patted me on the back and shook their heads, including my good friend Dan DeBlanc from New Orleans. Dan would go on to earn a silver star flying Cobra gunships.

"Rick, you are one lucky son of a bitch," Dan said. "You probably got your one crash out of the way and won't have another one."

That would not be the case.

That flight had been our last scheduled training. We were scheduled to ship out in two days. I needed to get back in the saddle and get some confidence back. I knew I was a pretty good pilot and that the accident had been caused in large part by the limitations of the aircraft and, more importantly, the wind. The gust that had pushed the big nose of the 34 ninety degrees to the right had pushed us past the point of no return. Nonetheless, I needed to fly again right away to clear the cobwebs and regain my confidence.

It wasn't to be. We were ordered to ship out two days later as planned.

I reported to the naval facility at Treasure Island in San Francisco and was escorted to the barracks. I'd spend the night there and fly out the next day to Guam, and then to Da Nang, South Vietnam. Surprisingly, I was the only one in the barracks. I sat on a cot in the cavernous room, contemplating what was behind, and what lay ahead. I felt as alone as I ever had.

The next day, I boarded a troop carrier for the long flight to Guam. It was a big C-130. I remember the seats were webbed and faced one another across the interior cargo hold. Thankfully, it was full. It was a long, uncomfortable flight, and we had to yell to be heard over the roar of the engines but talking to one another gave us some relief from our boredom and loneliness. We spent the night in Guam and left the next morning for Vietnam on another troop carrier.

Everyone I've ever talked to had the same first impression as they deplaned in Vietnam. As I grabbed my bag and climbed into the jeep that was to take me to the Marble Mountain airstrip next to Da Nang, I asked the driver, "What the hell is that smell?"

"Welcome to Vietnam, sir," the corporal said as he smiled. "That's the wonderful odor of burning shit. For the most part, there's no sewage system here. All the refuse from the latrines has to be burned in order to dispose of it. Nice, huh?"

I'd soon learn that the toilet facilities were the same as most U.S. campgrounds, with open pit toilets. Except in Vietnam, they usually had two seats that shared the same bench, with half of a fifty-gallon drum down below. The "outhouse" was a simple wooden box with screening on the top half. Every so often some poor Marine who'd made the mistake of breaking a rule or getting on the bad side of his company sergeant would find himself assigned to the "honey bucket brigade." That meant he and another transgressor got to drag out the two drums of shit, pour fuel on it, light it on fire, and stir the shit until all or most of it was consumed by the flames. It was an ongoing process, and as a result, every base always smelled like ... well, shit. It was always an extra treat when the wind blew toward the mess tent.

We arrived at the operations shack at the Marine airbase at Marble Mountain, just north of Da Nang. I entered the office and was greeted by the duty staff sergeant.

"Welcome to Vietnam, Lieutenant," he said with a wry smile. "What do you think so far?"

"Smells delightful."

"Yeah, that was my first impression too. Your orders are to report to HMM-362 up at Phu Bai. Be here at 0800 for your flight. The corporal will show you to your quarters." He looked up from his paperwork and stared directly into my eyes. "Good luck."

I presumed he knew I'd need it. He was right.

6

Phu Bai

The combat base at Phu Bai was situated along Highway 1, which ran the length of Vietnam. It was strategically located seventy miles south of the DMZ and ten miles south of the provincial city of Hue, which had been the site of one of the fiercest battles of the Vietnam War. On January 31, 1968, at the onset of the Tet Offensive, the Viet Cong and a division-size force of North Vietnamese regulars invaded and captured the city of Hue.

A variety of elements of the South Vietnamese army, the 1st Cavalry Division of the U.S. Army, and the 1st Battalion 1st Marine Regiment were involved in the counterattack. It took a month for the Marines to retake the city. Vastly outnumbered, the 1st Battalion 1st Marine Regiment, led by Lieutenant Colonel Ernie Cheatem, entered the city, and engaged the enemy in what proved to be one of the bloodiest battles of the war, involving ferocious house-to-house urban warfare.

Uncommon valor was a common occurrence during the bitter fighting. Five Medals of Honor eventually would be awarded to men who risked their lives to save the lives of their comrades, and in many cases, continued to lead and take the fight to the enemy.

What possesses a man like USMC Gunnery Sergeant John L. Canley, who, although wounded himself, ran through heavy enemy fire time and again to pull his wounded men to safety, and then continued to lead them, assaulting heavily fortified enemy positions?

What possesses men like USMC Staff Sergeant Alfredo Gonzales and U.S. Army Sergeant Joe Hooper, who although both severely wounded, still led their men toward the enemy under heavy fire and in many cases single-handedly overran their positions to engage and destroy them?

What possesses a man like Chief Warrant Officer Frederick Ferguson to ignore calls to stay out of a confined area and instead fly his helicopter through heavy antiaircraft fire and intense ground fire and rescue five members of another downed helicopter?

What possesses a man like U.S. Army Staff Sergeant Clifford Simms to throw himself on an exploding booby trap to save the lives of the men around him?

What possesses them is the heart of a lion, and the utter determination, no matter what the danger, to do what must be done. Each man in the battle of Hue gave no less, and it speaks to the true nature of the American soldier. I pray that the people of this country never forget this again—for decades, they did.

By the end of the battle, the city had been nearly destroyed. Marine and Army casualties were reported as 216 killed and 1,584 wounded. The South Vietnamese army, whose units were the first to respond to the attack, reported 457 killed and 2,123 wounded. The Viet Cong and North Vietnamese regulars estimated 5,000 killed and an unknown number of wounded.

Thousands of civilians died, most at the hands of the North Vietnamese. Mass graves around the city yielded more than 3,000 men, women, and children. They'd been executed or buried alive. The true toll will never be known. None of those facts were broadcast to the American public, as the mood of our involvement in the war took a turn for the worse. While it was a military victory for the U.S.-led forces, it would prove to be a turning point in the attitude of the American public and the media. People began to say the war couldn't be won, a fact that many years later would prove wholly inaccurate. Stay tuned.

The base at Phu Bai housed both the Marines and the Army's 82nd Airborne Division. The Marines occupied the east side of the single airstrip, and the Army had the west. Our side was a conglomeration of tents and flimsy wooden structures situated on a flat, featureless expanse of dirt and the finest sand you can imagine. When it rained, the sand was so fine the water just beaded up and ran off to the east. During the monsoon, we often couldn't fly and spent a lot of time cooped up in our hooches, reading or sleeping. The rain would create a fast-moving creek down the middle of the hooch, carrying away whatever was lying around. "Hey, Marine, your flip-flop is departing the area via the front door," often came the cry.

When the wind would blow, which was most days, the sand got into every conceivable nook and cranny. We simply couldn't keep it out of our eyes, ears, nose, throat ... or anywhere else. Keeping weapons and aircraft engines clean and operational was a constant battle in itself.

We lived in wooden huts with tin roofs. The walls were planks about three feet high, and the rest was screening up to the roofline to allow for some airflow in the stifling heat. Of course, that just let the sand blow in at will. We were lucky enough to have actual cots to sleep on with a sheet and blanket—not like those poor grunt bastards who lived in the jungle in the most horrendous conditions for weeks and months at a time. Every time I got fed up with my conditions, I'd remind myself what the Marines in the bush were going through.

Be thankful you aren't out there, Rick, I'd think to myself.

It was impossible to keep the sand out of your bed, no matter how tightly you made it up. I'd try to wipe the sand from my sheets before getting into bed, but inevitably I'd be up in the middle of the night, wiping out more sand, to little avail.

The mess tent was just that—a big tent with, yup, you guessed it, wooden walls, and screen siding. I'd write my name in the sand on my plate at the table to see if it was covered over with sand by the time I got to the mess line. It usually was. The food was horrible. It was so bad that at times we preferred the C-rations that the grunts in the field depended upon.

C-rats were cans of prepared meals, such as spaghetti and beef, or ham and lima beans, or perhaps a fruit cake. As grim as they were, they often were better than the mess tent's mystery meat and powdered mashed potatoes laden with saltpeter (potassium nitrate). I guess they had to keep all the testosterone in those twenty-year-old Marines in check somehow.

The guys in our hooch decided that if we were going to survive, we'd need to do some of our own cooking. First, we cut a fifty-gallon drum in half and used a heavy metal screen to make a barbecue. The next step of our plan involved the wonderful little Vietnamese woman who was our hooch maid. Han kept our hooch clean (no small feat with eight smelly Marine pilots) and did our laundry. She was basically a housemother to a bunch of fraternity boys. From time to time, we'd send Han into the town of Phu Bai to buy whatever looked good. I still remember the shrimp she'd come back with—they were the size of lobsters and just as good.

We also developed a discreet arrangement with the CO's cook, who would trade good scotch for decent steaks when he had them. It was probably a court-martial offense, but as we liked to say, "What are they going to do? Cut off my hair and send me to Vietnam?"

Each of the eight pilots in a hooch had a little cubicle that contained a cot, a footlocker, and a small metal locker. We hung up sheets for walls to achieve a modicum of privacy.

Across from my cubicle was Ron Janousek, who went by "Hauser." I loved his humor and constant smile, and we became best friends. Part of Ron's humor was his proficiency in the pranks department.

At one point during our tour, we were stationed for two months on the *Iwo Jima*, a helicopter carrier positioned just off the coast of Da Nang. During those operations, the carrier was approaching its ten-thousandth aircraft landing in a storied career that stretched back to World War II. It was a big deal, and the whole squadron was ordered into the air to take part, with our commanding officer, Colonel Schmidt, scheduled to make that landing himself.

Colonel Schmidt was a pompous asshole who spent most of his tour on junkets to Tokyo and Australia. When he was around, he was excellent at writing himself up for medals he didn't deserve in order to further his career, while the meat of the squadron did the dangerous flying. I loved the Marine Corps, and almost every other officer I met was outstanding, but I was appalled by Colonel Schmidt's lack of leadership and honor. He was a perfect target for Hauser.

Half the squadron had come in to land and when the ten-thousandth position was next, Ron declared a fuel emergency. "This is Yankee Lima 45," he called. "I have a low-fuel emergency and request immediate clearance to land."

My copilot, Steve "The Stick" Wilson, and I were still in the air, waiting for our turn to land. Steve looked over at me. "Holy shit," he said. "Ron's going to cut out the old man." Steve had earned his nickname because he was six foot four and at best, 140 pounds. Also, being a "good stick" meant you were a good pilot, and Steve would earn that reputation soon enough. "That boy has balls, I'll give him that. But I sure wouldn't want to be in his shoes when the CO gets down."

"This ought to be interesting," I said.

The landing officer on deck had no option but to let Ron land next.

The crew had set up a big ceremony to commemorate the landing. After Ron exited his aircraft, the captain of the *Iwo Jima* met him and shook his hand. As the rest of the aircraft landed, Ron was taken to the front of the flight deck, where all hands stood in attendance. When the ceremony began, Ron accepted his award from the captain with a huge smile on his face. Colonel Schmidt stood next to him, absolutely furious but unable to do anything but congratulate him as well. The look in his eye was pure anger as he shook Ron's hand. It was all the rest of the junior pilots could do to not burst out laughing. Ron was a legend afterward.

Next to me on the same side of the hooch was another good friend, Pete Peterson. An excellent pilot from Kenosha, Wisconsin, Pete loved to talk about hunting and fishing, something I enjoyed as well while growing up. We hit it off and spent a lot of down time together. He and Ron and I developed a great friendship. It was a bit trite to call us the Three Musketeers, but that was how we thought of ourselves.

At the end of most days, after a shower and some terrible mess tent

Lt. Ron Janousek (Hauser) being congratulated by the *Iwo Jima* CO for its 10,000th landing (author's collection).

food, the three of us would head off to the O Club to see how much we could drink. It was the only way we knew to decompress and try to relax.

That's where we headed at the end of the day when Yankee Lima 27 had been shot down in the mission to support the Marines of A and C companies. As we walked through the heat to the club, I asked Ron how his day had been.

"Not too bad today, pal. Spent most of the day doing some resupply runs and taxi service for the brass."

Not all our flying was difficult combat missions. In fact, many were somewhat routine, although anytime you flew, you were at risk.

I turned and asked, "How about you, Pete?"

"Spent most of my day up at the Z, hopping around," he said casually. Z stood for DMZ.

There was nothing casual about hopping around the DMZ, which was a series of tiny mountaintop LZs, always in range of mortar teams hidden in the mountainous and thick triple canopy of the jungle. In addition to lobbing the occasional round to mess with the poor Marines manning those horrendous outposts, the teams considered helicopters particularly juicy targets, so getting in and out quickly was advised.

Ron looked at me. "Heard you had a tough day, though."

"Yeah, it was a ballbuster. Cheated the Grim Reaper for sure."

That was about all we'd ever say about our days. No matter how easy or horrific they were, we just didn't dwell on them. We'd rather find some funny incident to laugh about.

In truth, we were in a system and a situation where we just were along for the ride, with no control over what happened. The overall operations of the war simply weren't part of thought processes. At least not in the early months. We were leaves floating down a river, being pushed wherever the current took us. We never discussed the validity of what was going on. We focused wholly on our missions, doing our jobs, and staying alive. It wasn't until many years later that I'd reflect on it all and develop my own opinions about the war, my part in it, and what it all meant to me.

That night, we continued toward the O Club, laughing, and talking about the day Ron had cut the CO out of the pattern on the *Iwo Jima*.

The O Club was—oh yeah, you guessed it—a big tent, with the same construction and same wonderful surroundings as every other building. The good thing was a drink only cost twenty-five cents of military script. The bad thing was that someone could buy the whole O Club a round for about twenty dollars. It wasn't unusual to see four or five drinks line up in front of you as the Vietnamese waitresses scurried about filling orders. My poison was vodka and orange juice—I figured the healthy orange juice minimized the damage of the vodka.

"Hey, Skewdwyba," one of the waitresses would call out. "Screwdriver" was their nickname for me because they had a hell of a time with the R in Rick. "You want 'notha' one?"

I'd look down at the glasses lined up in front of me and smile broadly. "Do I look like I need another one? Maybe you're trying to get me drunk and take me home, yes?"

They'd always smile back, exposing teeth blackened from the beetle bark they chewed. "No, Skewdwyba," they'd say, "you too ugly."

Really?

The boys were always a bit nervous about the location of the O Club—it was near the perimeter wire and had been blown up twice with mortar rounds. We just hoped someone had discovered the aiming stake and removed it. On one occasion, the perimeter guards caught two Viet Cong women crawling through the mud outside the wire with explosive satchels strapped to their backs, headed for the O Club. We all knew there was a decent chance we might not survive our tour, but I certainly hoped I'd go down in a more glorious fashion than drunk in the O Club. What would my relatives think about their war hero then? How embarrassing.

That evening, the club was full as usual, and the eight pilots from our hooch sat around and swapped stories. Luckily, all the pilots from our squadron had returned safely. Another squadron based at Phu Bai, HMM-364, the Purple Foxes, wasn't as lucky. They'd lost an aircraft and crew performing a recon (reconnaissance) extract in the treacherous jungle terrain east of An Hoa. A pilot from HMM-364 burst into the club with news of the loss.

It was a black day for the Purple Foxes, who'd drawn the rotating duty of recon inserts and extracts. It was common practice, whenever possible, to rotate the operations of recon inserts, medevacs, resupply duties, and admin runs among the various squadrons so that one squadron wasn't always being served shit sandwiches.

What was truly egregious about those recent recon operations was that those operations in that valley east of An Hoa had been suffering horrendous casualties, with multiple aircraft and crew losses. The major running the operations was trying to confirm and identify what he felt was a full NVA regiment in that area.

We all had the same opinion of that ill-conceived operation: *Guess what, Major? The fucking NVA regiment is there. How many more aircraft crews and recon Marines do you have to fucking lose before the light turns on?*

It wouldn't be the last time we'd question certain operational decisions. In fact, such questions would prove the foundation of tremendous frustration about what we were doing and what we were accomplishing as our time in Vietnam progressed.

The mood in the club changed from raucous laughter to dead silence. Not every pilot knew every other pilot in every squadron, but I'd flown with both of those pilots stateside. We'd flown together in Pensacola and spent our advanced combat training in Santa Ana together too. We'd flown, partied, and lived together for well over a year.

At Santa Ana, we were all still flying the H-34. Then the Marines told us two weeks before deployment that they'd decided to phase out the aging H-34 and its less-efficient reciprocating engine and employ the newer and stronger H-46 with its twin jet engines. The problem was that the Marines purchased their H-46s from the Navy, and we got the old A models. They were designed for ship-to-ship cargo transfer. Combat operations were much more demanding. Then there was the lack of protection for the pilots.

When they told us at Santa Ana about the scheduled phaseout, three of us went to the CO's office and pleaded our case to remain in the H-34. It was a contentious meeting. At last, the CO said, "All right, you sons of bitches, you stay in the 34 and get the hell out of my office."

The other two pilots deployed just before me, so I'm pretty sure I was the final Marine pilot to be deployed to Vietnam in the H-34. I'm positive that saved my life.

When I showed up as the last pilot to join the squadron, I became the traditional FNG—Fucking New Guy. It's a tag every new member of any unit receives until the next new guy comes along. There were no other new pilots to join HMM-362 after me, so I got to carry the inglorious handle for my full tour. It was okay, though, because I loved the H-34, and it was an honor to be the last FNG. Had I been transitioned into the H-46, my chances of surviving the war would have been small. The casualty rates for H-46 pilots in those days were significant.

The two pilots from HMM-364 who had just lost their lives were in the group of pilots that had remained behind in Santa Ana to be transitioned into the H-46. Fred Manson was a six-foot-four, 250-pound barrel-chested Marine who'd played football at Notre Dame and married his high school sweetheart. He talked about her endlessly. Back in Pensacola, when we'd go terrorize a nearby Air Force O Club at happy hour, Fred had no trouble cutting a path through the upset Air Force officers as our contingent of surly, discourteous Marines poured through the door. We loved causing a scene and pissing them off. We were young, and full of testosterone as well as a bit of an attitude. After all, we did have to uphold our reputation as Marines.

"You gentlemen don't mind if we clear a space at the bar, do you?" Fred would ask as he wedged himself between a couple of Air Force officers. "My friends here are really thirsty. They tend to get cranky if they don't start drinking by 1700 hours, and it's already 1715. Plus, we just love how nice the O Clubs are in the Air Force. And you have a better selection of good booze." He was too big to argue with, and his demeanor was more than intimidating. Generally, the bar area would clear out. It was always a ballbuster, for sure.

Dale Broussard was from La Grange, Louisiana, and had graduated from LSU before joining the Corps. We had a lot of parties at Pensacola, and we could always count on Dale to cook the best damn Cajun food we could imagine. Dale's parties were the best.

He was proud of his cooking and always liked to announce the menu. "Tonight, gentlemen, we're havin' my mutha's famous recipe fo' red beans and rice, along with some o' her delicious jambalaya. Y'all help yaselves and they's beer on the back porch."

We feasted on great food and drank ungodly amounts of beer to the sounds of zydeco music rocking the walls of the old, wood-framed house he'd rented.

My heart sank when I heard their names. I felt like someone had punched me in the stomach. Shit, we'd been sitting at the same table, drinking, and laughing, just the prior night. I stared at the table and tried to control my emotions. Chairs began scraping the floor as men pushed back from their tables and headed out of the club. I felt frozen in place. In a fog, I wandered outside with Ron and Pete and headed back to the hooch. No one said a word.

I spent a sleepless night thinking of all the great times flying and partying we'd shared. I prayed for the men and their families. I tried to process their loss. In the early hours of the morning, I worked on regaining my focus and strength of mind. I had to put everything into a pigeonhole and prepare to fly at razor edge's efficiency. Using the pigeonhole process was the only way to deal with much of what we had to deal with. Everything we compartmentalized would rear its ugly head decades later. But in the moment, I had to rely on my confidence as a pilot and the leadership skills I'd learned at Quantico and Pensacola.

7

Water Buffalo

It was another hot, miserable day in Phu Bai with a brisk wind blowing sand everywhere. With no flight operations scheduled, Hauser, Pete, Art Fanning, and I were sitting in our hooch drinking beer and shooting the breeze when a corporal from the squadron office knocked on the door.

"Permission to enter, sirs," came his voice through the screen door.

"Come on in, if you think it's safe," Art hollered.

The corporal pushed through the door, saluted, approached me, and handed me some paperwork. "Lieutenant, these are your orders to report to Subic Bay, Philippines, for jungle survival training."

"Oh, baby," chirped Hauser, who was sitting next to me. "Are you in for some fun!"

Everyone else was smiling and chuckling, which made me curious. "What kind of *fun* are we talking about?" I asked.

"Oh, you'll find out when you get there," Pete added with a big smile hanging under raised eyebrows. Art just looked over and smiled like a Cheshire cat.

Since I was the last pilot to join the squadron, everyone else had already been through the course at Subic. They obviously knew what was in store. Well, at least I would be out of Phu Bai, the heat, and the blowing sand for a week. *Couldn't be any worse, right?* I thought.

"Thanks, Corporal," I said.

"Sir, you are to report at 0800 at the airfield for a hop down to Da Nang."

"Thanks again.... I think," I replied, noticing that he, too, had a shit-ass grin on his face just like everyone else. He gave me a salute which I returned. Then he turned, exited back through the screen door, and headed back to the squadron office, head bowed against the wind, each step creating a cloud of dust as he plodded through the talcum powder fine sand outside.

"Okay, you assholes, tell me what's going on," I pleaded.

Nothing but grins and headshakes side to side.

"Okay fine. But I'm not bringing you bastards any gifts back."

"Yeah, well, just make sure you don't bring anything contagious back, pal," Hauser added followed by more grins and chuckles from Pete and Art.

• • •

The next morning, I grabbed my old military-issue canvas bag, stuffed it with enough clothes for a week, and hitched a ride to the flight line. There were four other pilots waiting at the H-53 that would take us down to Da Nang for our flight to Subic. I recognized two pilots, Dave Strickland and Roy Newsome, who were from HMM-364.

"Hey, guys. How you boys doin'?" I offered.

"Hey, Rick. You joinin' us on this little vacation?" Roy asked.

"Not sure about the vacation part, but yeah I'm tagging along."

I introduced myself to the other pilot, Tom Robinson, who was from HMM-161, and we walked up the ramp into the belly of the 46. I stuffed some earplugs in to mitigate what I knew was going to be a very noisy ride down to Da Nang. I loved flying helicopters, but I hated being in the belly of one. Kind of like being in a big metal trash can with someone beating on it from the outside with a baseball bat.

About an hour later, we disembarked at Da Nang, loaded ourselves and our bags into a couple of jeeps that were waiting for us, and headed off to the bachelor officers' quarters. We dumped our gear and then walked over to the officers' mess hall for some chow, which was surprisingly good. Of course, anything was better than the food at Phu Bai. We spent the rest of the day playing cards and shopping at the PX for things we could never get at Phu Bai. Da Nang, being one of the biggest bases in Vietnam, had a well-stocked store with just about anything you could want—including good scotch.

Well, hell, I thought. *This is a pretty good start. Good food, an air-conditioned room all to myself, an honest-to-God flush toilet, and a real bar at the officers' club. Life is good.* In the back of my mind, however, all I could see was the shit-eating grins of my pals as I left that morning.

The six of us headed to the officers' club for dinner about 1800. I almost felt I was back in the States as we were ushered to a table with a white tablecloth, real cloth napkins, shiny silverware, and a small vase of flowers in the middle.

How strange it is, I thought, looking at the table as we sat down, *that we forget the small things that give us pleasure and often take for granted until they are absent from us.* I vowed to never forget to appreciate those small things again when (if?) I returned home.

I ordered a T-bone steak, rare, with scalloped potatoes, green beans, and a Caesar salad, two martinis to wash it down, followed by a piece of peach pie and a snifter of cognac. I wondered how I might find a way to get transferred to Da Nang.

After dinner, we all headed to the bar and managed to put a respectable dent in their stock. I slept better that night than I had since I got in-country.

After a tasty breakfast the next morning, we loaded ourselves back into two jeeps and were driven out to the flight line, where we boarded a C-130 for our trip to the Philippines.

Nothing like an eleven-hour flight in the belly of a C-130 to drive you stir-crazy. Wonderful seats of canvas webbing, ear suppressors to help reduce the mind-numbing engine noise, terrible food, and no booze. I had almost forgotten how grueling the fifteen-hour flight had been from San Francisco to Guam aboard the C-130 when I left the United States for Vietnam three and a half months ago.

We arrived at Subic Bay late at night tired, cranky, and hungry. Walking down the back ramp, even at night, the heat and humidity was just like Vietnam. For a moment I wondered if we had turned around and were back in Da Nang.

I looked over at Roy. "I just hope the O Club bar is still open."

"Please, God," he responded.

The four of us were picked up on the tarmac by a World War II-vintage 6×6 troop truck with wooden bench seats and a canvas top. Probably left over from the U.S. occupation in 1944. Nice follow-up to the lovely seating on the C-130. We were driven to the BOQ, where we checked in only to find the bar was closed. That was why buying booze at the PX in Da Nang proved to be one of the more prudent decisions I had made so far on this trip. Hopefully, I would have a chance to replenish once we returned, because we made short order of my scotch that first night.

The next morning, the four of us reported to the headquarters admin office at 0800. A corporal walked us down the hall to a small classroom, where we were introduced to a master gunnery sergeant with enough combat and campaign ribbons on his big barrel chest to fill a small suitcase. Like all senior NCOs in the Marine Corps, his khaki uniform was starched, crisp, and looked like it had been sprayed on his chiseled six-foot-tall frame. His name tag above the chest pocket on the left side read *Strong*. He was that for sure, but I wondered if that was his given name, or he had changed it. Seemed contrived somehow. Nonetheless, it certainly fit him.

While as officers we outranked him, we were being addressed by a man who commanded our utmost respect. Gunnery sergeants in the Marine Corps are the backbone of the Corps. They have the strength, command presence, experience, determination, and fire in the belly that makes the Marine Corps the most feared and lethal fighting force on the planet. There isn't an officer in the field that doesn't look to and rely on his gunnery sergeants for advice and direction when necessary.

"Gentlemen." His raspy voice commanded our attention. "Please be seated. You will be spending the next three days in the jungle learning survival skills. You will be under the command of a team of Negrito tribesmen. The Negrito tribesmen have inhabited these islands for tens of thousands of years, and the jungle is their home. They were invaluable in the guerrilla resistance during the Japanese occupation in World War II. You will learn much from these brave, strong men. Listen and learn, because it may save your life in the event you are shot down and need to evade the enemy until rescued. Are there any questions?"

No one said a word. The thought of being shot down had always been in the back of our minds, but hearing it spoken aloud made the hair stand up on the back of my neck. I am sure I was not alone in that reaction.

"You will be given one small sack of rice and a canteen of water. Other than that, you will have to learn to live off of what the jungle can provide. Treat these men with the respect they deserve, and they will treat you the same. Be grateful that you have this opportunity to interact and learn from these resourceful and resilient men."

The gunny swept his steely gaze across each of us. The room was silent other than the sound of the air conditioner humming in the window.

"Return to your quarters, change into your fatigues, and reassemble out front of this admin building in one hour. Bring nothing else with you. You are dismissed."

We filed out after a brief, "Thank you, Gunny," from each of us.

One hour later, we boarded the same 6×6 troop truck and spent the next two hours bouncing along on the wooden bench seats inside the canvas-covered sweatbox on our way into the equatorial jungle of Luzon. It was probably in the 90s and terribly humid. Must have been over a hundred inside the 6×6.

It was midday when we turned off the paved highway onto a rutted dirt road for another miserable half hour before we came to our destination.

We climbed out of the 6×6 and tried to stretch out the kinks from the last two and a half hours of torture. We were standing on a wide spot in the road in the middle of dense, triple-canopy jungle when a staff sergeant and two very short black men emerged from the jungle. I assumed the black men were the Negrito tribesmen.

The sergeant, like the gunny back at Subic, was dressed in his starched khaki uniform with three rows of ribbons above his left shirt pocket and a nametag over the right that read *Reynolds*. He was about five and a half feet tall, thin, and wiry, with a pronounced, beak-like nose and piercing green eyes. I silently nicknamed him "Hawk."

How in God's name, I thought to myself, *does he keep his uniform in such perfect shape in this heat way the hell out here in the middle of nowhere?* But I shouldn't have been surprised. It is an obsessive trait for NCOs in the Marine Corps no matter where they are stationed. I am pretty sure one of the most important items in their luggage is a travel iron.

Sergeant Reynolds walked up to us, rendered a salute, which we all returned, and spoke. "Gentlemen, I am Sergeant Reynolds. I will be your liaison during the next three days of jungle survival training. These two men behind me will be your instructors. As you may or may not know, these men come from a tribe that has inhabited these jungles for thousands of years. They are a wealth of information, and hopefully you will retain all that they will teach you over the next three days. Your lives could depend on that."

The two men standing behind him were maybe four feet in height, black-skinned with aboriginal features. A thick head of dense coarse black hair framed their angular jaws and cheekbones set under heavy, thick eyebrows and dark, brooding eyes. Their shirtless, lean, muscular

71

frames gleamed in the sunlight. Each wore a large knife tucked into a waist sash that held up their rough cotton pants. They were very hard and fierce-looking men stepping out to meet us from a timeless chapter of Philippine history.

They surveyed us for several minutes without moving a muscle, then turned and motioned for us to follow them down a narrow path leading into the jungle. We looked over at Sergeant Reynolds, who jerked his head to the side. Clear enough. We followed the two Negrito tribesmen, with Sergeant Reynolds bringing up the rear.

The path eventually opened into a clearing, and there in the center was a camp with several small, thatched roof palapas circled around a central firepit. We were led to one of the larger palapas, where we were seated at a table. It didn't take long to realize that everything—and I mean everything—in the camp was fashioned from bamboo. The four of us sat at the table, the top of which was made from inch-wide strips of bamboo eight feet long lashed together with bamboo webbing.

It was truly amazing. The palapas, the thatched roofs, tables, chairs, stools, spoons, forks, knives, plates, bowls, hammocks, everything from bamboo. What was even more amazing was that these men had only one tool. It was a handmade bolo knife fashioned, in this case, from the flyleaf suspension plate of a Ford truck. In fact, the one I saw still had part of the stamped letters F O R D on the blade. The knife was about eighteen inches long, with a wide, flat middle reducing to a narrower tip and sharp point on the end. The handle was made of bone.

Bamboo grows in sections, each separated by a solid partition. The sections are called nodes, and the partitions are called internodes. By cutting an eight-inch-wide piece of bamboo below the internode and again a few inches above, you have a ready-made bowl. Cut a little shallower, and you have a plate. Make two vertical cuts down one side of a node, and you can fashion a knife, spoon, or fork from that piece. Cutting thin strips from the skin of the bamboo produces straps that can be woven into baskets, hammocks, or lashing for strapping together a palapa. One tool and some good-sized pieces of bamboo, and these guys seemed to be able to make just about anything.

As we were taking all of this in, Sergeant Reynolds approached the table. "Gentlemen," he addressed us, "you will be leaving here in about thirty minutes. You will be given one canteen of water and a small bag of rice. Over the next three days, your instructors will show you how to feed yourselves with what the jungle can provide. At the risk of repeating myself, what you will learn from these men could save your life one day."

He then motioned to the two Negritos standing just outside the palapa to step forward in front of our table. He introduced each from left to right.

"Gentlemen, this is Tibu and his brother, Tarek. They speak a bit of English, so you should have no problem communicating. So unless anyone has any questions, your canteens and rice bags are on the table outside. See you in three days," he added before rendering a salute, which we all returned.

I thought of a few smart-ass remarks, but somehow they didn't seem like a good idea given the importance of what we were about to undertake. Growing up, I had always been fascinated by stories of war and, in particular, those about prisoner of war camps, escape and survival. I was particularly intrigued by the story of Dieter Dengler, a Navy fighter pilot who was shot down in Laos in 1966, captured, tortured, and managed to escape, spending twenty-three days on the run before being rescued. One of the things I remember the most was that Dieter was able to survive in captivity because he was willing to eat things others could not. Kept in a bamboo cage and at times partially submerged in water, he had to eat rats and even maggots from the open wounds he had sustained. He survived because of his mental toughness. I always wondered if I would have that same determination and strength of will if I found myself in a similar situation. Could I bring myself to eat something so disgusting in order to survive? Well, I would soon have a chance to answer that question.

We picked up our canteens and rice, looked at each other with raised eyebrows, and followed our two Negrito tribesmen down a path on the far side of the camp. The jungle enveloped us immediately, triple-canopy trees blocking out most of the sun except for occasional breaks in the green ceiling over us. We walked for maybe an hour without speaking, taking in our equatorial surroundings and the incredible variety of trees and vegetation around us. Every so often, we passed through a huge stand of bamboo, some of which were perhaps a foot in diameter. Periodically, sunlight briefly filtered through the dense canopy overhead, producing dust-filled golden shafts of light penetrating down to the fern-covered jungle floor below.

The Philippine jungle is rich not only in abundant vegetation, but also animal life. As we ventured deeper and deeper into the jungle, the eerie cry of the peacock pheasant, the dog-like bark of the great hornbill, and the screech of the macaque monkey combined to unnerve and remind us that we were in an environment that was certainly beautiful yet foreboding in some visceral way. The local wildlife was ushering us into their world as we left ours behind. I felt small and terribly insignificant as we marched forward farther and farther into the belly of the Luzon wilderness.

At one point, Tibu, the lead Negrito, stopped and signaled for us to gather around him. He pointed to a number of thick vines that looked like bark-covered tendrils hanging from a huge hardwood tree next to the path. "Water," he said, pointing to one. He grabbed the vine and, with one quick swipe of his bolo, cut it in half. Out came a trickle of water which he drank, holding the opened vine above his mouth. "Not all trees make water. Rememba what dis tree look like," he said in his pidgin English. He cut more vines, and we all took a turn drinking from them. The water was surprisingly clean tasting. Lesson One.

We spent the rest of that first day walking and learning which plants were edible and which were poisonous. We gathered leaves to make tea later that night. He showed us lichen moss on the base of some trees that could be used as a poultice for cuts or wounds.

We stopped again, sometime in the late afternoon, I think. Without being able to tell the exact location of the sun under the thick jungle canopy, time seemed uncertain. We had not eaten since breakfast, and as our hunger grew, our thinking was beginning to be dominated by the thought of food. We were seated on the ground in a small clearing next to a tiny creek.

"You gettin' hungry, yes?" he asked. "You must learn to find food in the jungle and to control your mind at the same time. Accept that hunger is part of your situation. Just like you must endure pain, you must learn to endure hunger. There is food in this creek. There are small shrimp, bugs, and worms. I will show you how to find them."

Roy and Dave looked at me, and Roy mouthed a silent *"Bugs?"*

I answered with a small silent shudder and then licked my lips and patted my stomach. "Yum," I said.

Tibu proceeded to make a small dam across the creek using stones and mud from the creek bottom. He constructed the dam in such a way as to divert the water from its original path. Eventually the creek bed below dried up to a small, wet, muddy trench. He picked through the mud among the stones and debris and gathered four or five freshwater shrimp, some slugs, and a few water beetles. After cutting a section of bamboo from a plant nearby, leaving the bottom internode intact and cutting the top one away, he deposited the shrimp, slugs, and beetles into the bamboo container. Lesson Two.

We continued our march through the jungle, and again he halted to show us a tree with round, spiked fruit hanging in twos and threes.

"Durian," Tibu said.

He cut down several and opened them up, handing each of us a half. We devoured the fruit inside the hard outer shell. Not much of a lunch, but better than nothing. Half an hour later, he stopped again and pointed to a different tree with clusters of small yellow walnut-sized fruits.

"Duku," he remarked.

Again, he harvested several clusters and gave each of us a handful. It had a thin outer skin and soft, opaque, very sweet inner fruit. Lesson Three.

As the afternoon wore on, we stopped several times as Tibu pointed out different vegetation, the leaves of which were edible. He gathered handfuls of these and placed them in a small rucksack he had strapped to his back. The sunlight began to fade just as we came to another clearing in the jungle.

"We camp here tonight," Tibu said. "My brother will show you how to make bed."

Within a few minutes, Tarek had cut palm fronds and placed them in a pile. Next he cut one-inch-wide strips of bamboo about six feet long and lashed those together with thin strips of bamboo shaved from the outside of the same longer pieces. It was like a small wooden raft. They lashed together the palm fronds the same way and *voila*, jungle cot. Lesson Four.

The next amazing lesson was in fire making. For the first time, Tarek spoke. "I show you how make fire. Sit here." He pointed to the ground next to him. We did, glad to have anywhere to sit after walking all day.

He cut a three-foot section of bamboo about six inches in diameter. Then he split it down the middle, producing two half-round sections. Moving the point of his bolo in a circular fashion, he made a small, funnel-shaped hole in the bottom of one of the bamboo half-round sections, making sure to create only a pin-sized hole to the outside. Then he made a crosscut on the outside of that same section right over the pin-sized hole he had made from the inside. Next he chose an older dead piece of bamboo and, by moving the edge of the bolo blade up and down, scraped together a handful of very fine bamboo shavings which would serve as the tinder for the fire. He then carved a sharp edge on one side of the other three-foot sections of bamboo. He placed the tinder in the section with the hole in it. He then took the other section and put one end in the ground and the other against his belt. Leaning over, he placed the section with the crosscut in it on the sharp edge of the other section.

He began to push the piece with the crosscut back and forth on the sharp edge of the section in the ground. The friction began to turn the crosscut itself black, and smoke arose as the friction increased. Eventually the heat created embers in the tinder. He removed the tinder with the burning embers and began blowing on them to ignite a flame, which he placed under some dry leaves and twigs. We had a fire, and amazingly it only took him ten minutes from start to finish. Lesson Five.

Once we had a nice little fire going, Tibu cut another three-foot section of bamboo maybe four inches in diameter. He cut the top internode away and packed the remaining bamboo tube with rice and added some water from his canteen. Then he added more water to the other tube containing the shrimp, slugs, and beetles he had gathered from the stream earlier. He placed two forked branches into the ground on either side of the fire and placed the two bamboo tubes inside the forked section over the fire. Occasionally he would rotate the tubes as their contents cooked.

We waited, watching, and occasionally looking at each other rolling our eyeballs. As questionable as the food Tibu had harvested from the creek was, we were hungry enough not to care.

Finally, Tibu took the two bamboo tubes from their perch above the fire and, with his bolo, cut down lengthwise through each. There in the trough of one was cooked rice and the boiled shrimp, slugs, and beetles in the other. He doled out portions to each of us into our bamboo bowls we had cut for ourselves while dinner was cooking. The protein mixed with the white rice yielded a dark brown/black gruel. It tasted about how it looked.

As we were finishing our meager meal, Tibu addressed us. "Today you learned how to find water, food, make a fire, and cook a meal. But if you are evading the enemy, you will not be able to make a fire. You will have to eat these little animals raw. That is something you will have to will yourself to do. Some men can and some cannot. Those that can, may survive. Those that cannot, will not survive."

I thought, *Man, I hope we don't have to try the raw option on this trip.*

That night we slept close to the fire to keep the mosquitos at bay. But it was a fitful sleep at best, especially given the fact that a group of macaque monkeys serenaded us most of the night with constant screeching and barking. We awoke early, smelling of campfire smoke, itching from bug bites, dirty, and hungry. Breakfast consisted of some more durian and duku fruit gathered by Tibu, and a tea made from some of the leaves he had picked earlier.

Well, what did I expect? I asked myself. *After all, it is survival training.* All I could think of was the chow I had enjoyed at the Da Nang officers' club just a couple of days ago. *I hope I get another shot at that food on the return trip.* I know it sounds like I was obsessed with food, but when it is bad or scarce, that is where the mind wanders. Well, at least mine does.

After our sumptuous breakfast, we headed out again, following Tibu down a narrow, well-traveled path with his brother bringing up the rear. As tired and hungry as I was, I had to admire the beauty and diversity of the jungle around us. Occasionally the humid dank air gave way to a wisp of fragrance from some unknown jungle flower. Calls and cries from the local inhabitants echoed through the trees, announcing our arrival to their neighbors ahead.

We had been walking for some time when we came across another small stream and stopped to rest and clean away the soot and smell from last night's fire. We were seated on some rocks next to the streambed when Tibu let out a shout. In his native tongue, he was calling his brother to come. Although I could not understand what he was saying, it was obvious he was alarmed about something. Tarek scurried past us headed for Tibu, who was just a few meters downstream. There was a lot of excited chatter going on amid some thrashing about in the undergrowth. I had started down the path when Tarek appeared and motioned for me to go back.

Suddenly there was Tibu holding a four-foot-long snake he had just killed. Like most people, I hate snakes, and the realization that these bad boys were around gave me the willies.

"Cobra," Tarek said. "Very dangerous. One bite, you die."

Well, that's comforting, I thought to myself.

Dave, who was from Mississippi and went by that nickname, chimed up. "Seen a lotta cottonmouths and rattlers, but neva seen a cobra before. I read that a spittin' cobra can blind a man from several feet away if he gets you in the eyes."

"Yeah, well, I don't plan on starin' at one should I come across one," Roy replied.

"Oh, you won't have to stare at him, pal," Dave said with a smirk. "He'll see you way befo' you see him, fo' sure."

Tarek put the snake in his rucksack. There was no doubt what we would be dining on tonight. We finished cleaning up and headed back down the path, stepping a bit more gingerly than before with eyes scanning the ground and forgoing looking around at the jungle.

We stopped somewhere around the middle of the day to rest and eat some more fruit Tibu and Tarek had found. Not much sustenance for the energy we were expending. Hunger now began to dominate our minds. My stomach ached, my feet ached, my back ached, and my head ached. No one was cracking any jokes now. All I could think of was food.

As if reading our minds, Tibu's voice stirred us from our lethargy. "If you are evading the enemy, you cannot let your mind wander. You must be alert and listen for any sound. You must keep moving at all costs. Stop only at night unless you can find good cover."

The reality of what might be required if we were shot down and had to evade and survive in the jungle began to settle in.

That night, we made our own beds as we had been taught and watched again as Tarek made preparations for a fire. Each of us took turns pushing and pulling the bamboo section with the tinder back and forth on the other bamboo section in order to create the friction necessary to ignite the tinder. It took a lot more energy and coordination than it looked like when Tarek had done this the previous night. I tried, then Roy tried—and not until the fourth of us tried did we create enough friction to ignite the tinder. Knowing what to do is one thing; being able to do it is another.

Tibu took out the snake from his bag, cut off the head and tail, skinned it, removed the entrails, cut the body into two-inch sections, and stacked them onto two bamboo skewers. He had Roy cut a piece of bamboo for the rice and put rice and water in that section. We cooked the rice and snake over the fire, mixing them together to make the snake more edible. "Barely edible" would be more accurate.

We spent another uncomfortable night next to the fire to ward off

78

as many mosquitoes as possible. What kept me going was the knowledge that we only had one more day of this before our "training" was over. I kept thinking of Dieter Dengler, who had no rice, no canteen of water, and no fire but had managed to elude the enemy that was out in force searching for him for twenty-three days. Twenty-three ... not three.

Morning of day three. Breakfast of tea and fruit. Just one more day. Light at the end of the tunnel.

We broke camp and set off following Tibu with Tarek bringing up the rear. The deeper we got into the jungle, the bigger the trees and the less dense undergrowth became. The trail widened out as the huge trees spread a solid canopy over us. It felt like we were walking through a jungle cathedral.

At one point, Tibu motioned for us to stop. He was staring up into the canopy overhead. When we looked up, I could see what looked like a lot of long orange pods hanging from the branches of these huge hardwood trees around us. To our surprise, Tibu and Tarek took out two large wooden handmade slingshots from one of their rucksacks. They placed what looked like marble-sized ball bearings in each slingshot and simultaneously aimed and fired up into the hanging orange pods. In an instant, what little sunlight was filtering through the jungle canopy was blotted out as thousands of huge bats with three-foot wingspans exploded out of the trees above, raining down a torrent of guano on and around us. Tibu and Tarek had scored direct hits, bringing down two of these huge jungle bats with bodies the size of squirrels. Bats may be one of the ugliest animals on the planet, and the thought of eating one was more than repulsive. This was going to really test our resolve. We all looked at each other with blank stares, lost in our own thoughts about how we were going to deal with this challenge later that day.

We found some more water vines, and each took our turns harvesting a mouthful, gaining some relief from the heat. We still had about half a canteen of water left, but that had to be rationed for the three days we were out here, so the water we could find from the vines was very important.

We spent the remainder of the day following our Negrito instructors, looking for fruit and gathering some leaves of various bushes they pointed out to us.

By evening, we had prepared another camp, collected water from a small stream we came upon, and cut bamboo for the fire preparation. Tarek took the two bats out of his rucksack and began to process them for cooking. He removed the wings, head, and feet, skinned the bodies, and removed the entrails. Watching this did not help my appetite no matter how hungry I was, and I was as hungry and tired as I had ever been. Tarek butterflied the remaining bodies of the bats and pushed a bamboo skewer through each lengthwise.

Sitting around the fire that night, our bamboo plates were full of rice, some greens that had been boiled, and pieces of grilled bat. Feast fit for a king. We looked at our plates, then at each other. Who would go first? *Hell,* I thought. *It's not going to kill me. If I can't do this now, it might kill me later.* I picked up one piece and took a bite. It was horrible, tough, and gamey. I scooped up some rice and greens with my fingers, put them in my mouth and began to chew. Everyone looked at me, wondering if I was going to spit the whole concoction out. I made a face of disgust but continued to chew until I was able to swallow, followed by a swig of tea. Well, I didn't throw up, so everyone else followed suit with a mixture of results.

Dave Strickland took one bite and spit it out. "I'm not eatin' that shit no matter how fucking hungry I am. We go back to base tomorrow, and I can make that."

I took another bite and managed to get it down with more rice and greens. Roy made it through two bites and quit. Tom Robinson from HMM-161 did the same. Just to be a real asshole, I made it through two more portions.

"Absolutely delicious," I said, forcing a smile while chewing my final bite. "Too bad there were only two bats," I quipped.

"Fuck off, Rick," Roy said. Dave and Tom gave me the international middle finger salute.

More tea … a lot more tea, and I waited to see how my body was going to process what I had just put into it. I got my answer in the middle of the night.

The morning of the fourth day. Miserable. Stomach cramps, filthy, bug-bitten, body sore, and in a really foul mood. Some tea and fruit, and we were on our way again. We walked about an hour. The jungle became denser and the trail narrower. Then we emerged into a clearing, and there in front of us was the camp we had left three days ago. Sergeant Reynolds was standing there in his crisp, clean, freshly pressed uniform.

"Did you gentlemen enjoy your camping trip?" he asked with a hint of a smile.

7. Water Buffalo

"Do we fucking look like we enjoyed ourselves, Sergeant?" Roy spat out.

"Well, you look a little worse for wear, but I do hope you learned something of value," he replied, still sporting a grin.

"Yeah, I learned I don't like bat," was all Roy could add.

I couldn't help myself. "Well, I found it a bit chewy, and it could have used a nice hollandaise sauce, but other than that, I found it passable."

"Fuck you, Gehweiler," Dave chimed in.

"Now, now, Dave," I said, "don't get your knickers in a wad just because you don't have an educated palate." I was really pushing the envelope at this point.

"All right, gentlemen," Sergeant Reynolds interrupted. "Your ride is waiting to take you back to base. I imagine you might want a shower and some real food. Be careful, though. Your stomachs have shrunk, so don't overdo it. That will only lead to more discomfort. Just a suggestion." Then his smile disappeared, and, with a more serious expression, he added, "Take care of yourselves back in Nam. Good luck, and I hope you never have to use what you learned here." He stepped back and gave us a sharp salute, which we returned with a nod of appreciation and a "thank you, Sergeant."

We turned to go, and there was Tibu and Tarek standing side by side. For the first time, we saw a smile on their faces. How many times had they taken men like us out on this three-day trek? Countless, no doubt. I looked at the others, and we came to attention and gave them a salute as well. Huge grins lit up their faces, and they each gave us a salute in return. It was a cool moment that I never forgot.

We climbed into the same shitty 6×6 truck for the 2½-hour ride back to the base at Subic. By the time it pulled up in front of the BOQ, we were four very dirty, tired, and cranky sons of bitches. That shower was one of the best I can ever remember enjoying. My fatigues were so filthy I thought of throwing them away, but a Filipino orderly came by, collected them, and said they would be ready by morning. I was starving, but I was more tired than hungry, so I just did a face-plant on the bed.

I awoke two hours later, got up, took another shower, changed into my khaki uniform, and went in search of my campmates. I found them where you might expect. At the bar. We ordered burgers and beers and made plans for the rest of the day and night. We were to depart the next

81

morning at 0800 for our flight back to Da Nang, which left us the rest of the day and night to have some fun.

Subic Bay was one of the biggest naval bases in the Pacific. It was manned by thousands of Navy and Marine personnel. Like most military bases, there was a town just off base that served the needs of the base population. The town outside of Subic was called Olongapo. It had a reputation for having more bars and brothels than anywhere in the Pacific theater.

Four young Marine helicopter pilots with three months of flying combat missions in Vietnam and three days with Tibu and Tarek in the jungle—not much doubt as to where we headed after lunch at the BOQ. We took a jeep to the front gate and walked through. Just a short walk, and we came upon a narrow footbridge leading into the town. The bridge spanned what was the nastiest, smelliest piece of water I had ever seen, an ink-black open sewer that flowed southward to Subic Bay. Small children were swimming in this cesspool and diving for coins thrown by the military people crossing over. I couldn't believe my eyes. I can still see that movie scene playing over and over even today.

"Jesus Christ," I said to Roy. "Those kids aren't going to live long swimming in that shit. What are these assholes doing throwing coins into that sewer and watching these kids dive for them? Unbelievable!"

As we were standing there watching this, a sailor in uniform tossed a handful of coins into the water.

"Hey, asshole!" I shouted. "What the fuck are you doing?"

He turned and looked at me as if I were from Mars. "Ain't no law against it, Lieutenant ... sir," he growled, drawing out the "sir" to mock me. "Hell, they need the money anyway," he added with a smirk.

"How about I throw *your* ass in that river, you piece of shit," I snapped back.

"Oh, I think that might be a court martial offense, Lieutenant," he replied with a syrupy drawl. "You know, big bad Marine officer picking on a poor enlisted sailor. Yeah, that might go bad for you."

I took two steps toward him before Roy grabbed my arm and pulled me back. "Let the asshole go, Rick. Not worth it," he said in a low voice.

"Better listen to your friend there, Lieutenant," the jackass said.

My blood was really boiling at this point. With an outstretched arm, I pointed my finger at him. "I'm gonna look for you in town, asshole, and if I find you, I'm going to drag your sorry ass into the nearest alley and beat that smirk off your face with the arm I rip from your

A hooch destroyed by a 122mm rocket (author's collection).

sorry-ass body. Now get the fuck off this bridge, and that is a direct order ... sailor boy."

He glowered back, turned, and shuffled away without another word.

"Come on, Rick," Dave offered. "Shake it off and let's go have some fun."

"Yeah, sure," I answered. "What a dick that shithead is."

We spent the next few hours walking through the narrow sleazy streets and alleys of Olongapo. One bar and brothel after another interlaced with a few open-front shops selling everything under the sun. The streets were filled with trash and garbage, and the smell of sewage hung like a heavy weight in the air.

A hooch destroyed by a 122mm rocket next to ours (author's collection).

The bars were full of young girls hawking their talents to everyone that entered. Yeah, well, not my cup of tea no matter how deprived I felt. There was probably enough disease in that town to wipe out the whole Marine Corps, and I wasn't going to risk contracting anything that I might have to deal with the rest of my life. The admonitions from my pals back at Phu Bai were clearer by now. The scene at the bridge and the filth of the town had me in a dour mood.

We barhopped for a few hours, and eventually the alcohol put me in a better mood.

Later that night, during one of our strolls around town, I found a shop that had some carved wood pieces, one of which caught my eye. I left the other guys outside and went in. There, just inside the door to

84

Pete (right) and me inside a destroyed hooch (author's collection).

the shop, was a beautiful water buffalo carved out of one solid piece of heavy monkey wood. It was a rich brown color, about two feet in height, three feet long, weighing about fifty pounds. I couldn't resist it. I had seen scores of these iconic animals from the air as they plowed the myriad of rice paddies below me with their owners guiding the hand plow from behind. As much as the mule was part of the plowing process in the small farms across America decades ago, the water buffalo was, and still is, the same for the Vietnamese farmer. To this day, it is considered the unofficial national animal of Vietnam.

As I looked down at this simple, hand-carved piece, I knew I had to have it. Somehow to me it represented my connection with Vietnam, and I wanted to have something physical to take home to remind me of my time there. So I paid whatever it was and asked them to ship it back to the United States for me.

"We don't ship anything, sir," the shop owner told me.

What? *Probably should have asked about that first, Rick,* I thought to myself. *What the hell am I going to do with this thing now?*

"Well, okay, box it up, and I guess I'll take it with me," I said to the owner.

He took two big cardboard boxes and cut them up to make one box and bound the whole thing up with a piece of hemp rope. There was no easy way to carry the darn thing other than hoist it up on one shoulder and hump it back to the base.

"What the hell is that?" Roy asked as I came out of the shop carrying this makeshift cardboard box on my shoulder.

"It's a fucking water buffalo, and I thought they would ship the damn thing for me. Apparently, that is not how they do things here. Christ, does everyone have to haul all the shit they buy here with them?" I ranted to no one in particular.

"Love to help you there, Rick," Dave said through his sappy grin, "but it looks like a one-man job to me. Maybe you should have bought something smaller, like a stuffed toy buffalo."

Off we went, working our way back to the base, me looking like Atlas with the world globe on his shoulder. After several stops to catch my breath and get some feeling back in my shoulder, we finally made it back to the BOQ. One last drink at the bar, and we headed to our rooms for the night.

The next morning, we arrived at the operations building at the Subic airbase to board our flight back to Da Nang. The C-130 was parked on the tarmac about a quarter mile away. The Navy ensign in the office told us that there were no vehicles available at the moment to take us out to the aircraft, so we would have to walk. I had my suitcase in one hand and the damn water buffalo in the cardboard box, which was already starting to fall apart, on my shoulder. By the time I stumbled up the ramp of the C-130, I was bathed in sweat, I had no feeling in my shoulder or right arm, the box had disintegrated, and my back felt like someone had beaten me with a bat.

Another glorious eleven-hour flight back to Da Nang, and we were all back in-country. The familiar smell of burning shit greeted us as we disembarked. Ah, home sweet home. No layover in Da Nang this time, as we were immediately escorted to a waiting H-46 for the short hop back to Phu Bai. Mercifully, we were picked up by two jeeps and taken to our hooches, me with my newfound friend in tow.

With no flight operations scheduled due to bad weather, I had a chance to recover from the three days in the jungle, but more importantly from my ordeal hauling the damn water buffalo all over the map. I placed him at the foot of my bed.

The next morning, Han, our hooch maid, came in and immediately upon seeing the carved buffalo, broke into a huge grin. She came shuffling over, mumbling excitedly something in Vietnamese and began petting the buffalo. She looked up at me with her black-tooth grin and said, "This very good luck. This good."

Every day for the rest of my tour, she would come in clean the hooch, do our laundry, and stroke that buffalo like it was her pet, repeating a word which sounded like "Dao" to me. I never found out what that word was or meant, but she said it with such fondness that it was obviously a term of endearment to her.

That buffalo sits in my office today. I named it Dao. It reminds me of and keeps me connected to my time in Vietnam. It brought me luck in that I made it back home. When I look at Dao today, I think of Vietnam, the people, my experiences there, the friends I lost, and of course Han. I wonder and worry about her. I wonder if or how she survived after the United States withdrew from that war and left the population we promised to protect at the mercy of the reprisals from the North Vietnamese.

8

The Sikorsky Bounce

South Vietnam was divided into four geographical areas called Corps Tactical Zones. I Corps was the most northern sector, stretching from the DMZ to an area south of Chu Lai. The 1st and 3rd Marine Divisions, the 1st Marine Air Wing, and various units from the Army's 101st Airborne were responsible for operations in I Corps. The DMZ was a cross-section of the country separating North and South Vietnam. Even though it was called demilitarized, that was hardly the case. Occupied by the North Vietnamese Army, it served as a launching point for attacks into the south.

One of the largest battles of the war was fought at the Marine base at Khe Sanh. The base was strategically located in the northwest corner of the country, bordering both the DMZ and the border with Laos, through which the Ho Chi Minh Trail ran. Twenty thousand North Vietnamese troops invaded the South during the Tet Offensive in January 1968 and surrounded the six thousand Marines based at Khe Sanh. The siege lasted seventy-seven days, during which time the Marines were under constant artillery and rocket bombardment from the hills and mountains to the north of the base. The fire from the mountains was so deadly that the C-130 cargo planes that were bringing in critically needed supplies and ammo came in with their rear ramps down. They'd land but continue rolling down the runway as the crew pushed out the cargo. Then they'd take off again under a hail of rocket and artillery shells. By the end of the siege, each side of the airstrip at Khe Sanh was littered with the wreckage of C-130s and helicopters.

In response to the siege, the United States began Operation Niagara, a campaign of unrelenting air bombardment directed at the surrounding enemy forces. Several hundred missions were conducted each day, and thousands of tons of ordnances fell from Navy, Marine, and Air Force bombers, as well as blanket bombing from B-52s. Eventually the siege was broken. The North Vietnamese, who had committed more than forty thousand men to the effort, abandoned the fight and retreated. The North Vietnamese, however, continued to occupy the DMZ, from which they could continue to support smaller operations in the south.

Being stationed at Phu Bai, just south of the DMZ, HMM-362 often flew missions in that area. It made for some interesting days, to be sure.

In Vietnam, all days seemed the same. There was no difference between weekdays and weekends. War doesn't take the weekends off. Time wasn't framed that way. However, on this one day, I remember it was a Sunday because a few of us had attended an early morning service at the base chapel and were sitting in the operations shack awaiting orders. I wasn't a particularly religious person, but I figured I could use all the help I could get. Plus, the sense of peace during the service had a calming effect on me. Calm is good.

The pilots and copilots assigned to fly that day were crammed into the operations shack, awaiting orders. The operations shack was just that: a typical rectangle building constructed of wooden walls and screening with a tin roof. At the far end from the entrance was the operations officer's office. In front of that door was the desk of the sergeant assisting the operations officer. The rest of the space was filled with an assortment of tables and chairs. That day, there were twelve hot and sweaty men assembled in the sweatbox. A couple of overhead fans slowly moved the hot air around. By eight o'clock, it was cooking.

Hauser, Pete Peterson, and I were playing gin while other pilots and copilots milled around. The air was thick and humid. The cards were soaked with sweat and stuck to the table. Flies buzzed around, hoping for any leftover morsel. Like many in the squadron, all three of us had gone through flight school at Pensacola together and spent eight weeks in Santa Ana as well.

"What duty do you think we're gonna draw today, guys?" Pete asked, looking up from his cards. "I'm hoping I get a few nice admin runs. Taxi driver for some brass making rounds."

"Yeah, good luck with that, Pete," Hauser said. "We haven't had a cruise day like that in a month. I'm bettin' it's the Z today for sure."

"Just as long as it isn't a fucking recon mission," I said.

Recon missions were notoriously dangerous—just ask the pilots from the Purple Foxes. Word was that the major who'd been sending in all those recon units had been relieved of his command. Good news for the future. Not in time for many good men, however.

The operations officer, Major Styles, was a decent guy with a big handlebar mustache. He made his way around the room, handing out our missions for the day.

Pete didn't get his admin run. He was assigned to resupply some of the firebases on the hills south of Khe Sanh. Hauser was to head to Camp Carroll, another firebase near Khe Sanh, and stand by for medevac duty. I was going to work out of what was left of Khe Sanh and ferry replacements and supplies to a number of hilltop LZs on the edge of the DMZ.

Just another day at the office.

I grabbed my gear—my M79 grenade launcher and a bandolier of grenades—and headed out with my copilot. Every pilot had his own weapon of choice to carry in his helicopter. The government-issued weapon for a pilot was a .38. That was good enough to shoot yourself with, but not much else. Most of us put it in our crotch while flying as extra protection for the boys against rounds coming through the floorboard.

I carried the M79, which is a short, fat, singled-barreled weapon that could launch a grenade similar to a can of soup a hundred yards or so. I figured if I got shot down, I wanted to make those sons of bitches think twice about coming for me. Plus, it was small and easily fit in the cockpit. I also carried my trusty .45 in case things did get up close and personal.

My copilot that day was Steve Delany, an Irish kid from Syracuse, New York. I was Irish and had been born in Syracuse, so we hit it off. Steve had been in-country six months when he'd graduated from copilot to pilot, or HAC (helicopter aircraft commander).

While Steve and I knew one another, we hadn't flown together. I figured that after three months as a copilot and another three as an HAC, he had to be good. I hoped so, anyway. A helicopter has two pilots in case one somehow becomes incapacitated—lead poisoning, for example.

Six flight crews headed out to our 34s, parked on the metal mats used for the staging area. It was only eight-thirty, but the heat coming from those mats already was enough to fry an egg—if we'd had any eggs. I checked with my crew chief and gunner, who were waiting for us.

Pilots were rarely assigned to the same aircraft every day, but the crew chief and gunner were permanently assigned to theirs. They were a team, and responsible for the maintenance and flying integrity of that particular aircraft. Our crew chief that day was Fred Dickson, a stout blond kid from Birmingham, Alabama, and Sonny Watson, from Dallas, Texas. A couple of good ol' southern boys with the accents to prove it.

"How you boys doing today?" I asked, looking at Fred.

"Jus' fine, LT," Fred drawled, using shorthand for *lieutenant.* "How 'bout you, suh?"

"Just dandy, Sergeant," I joked. "Thanks for asking. How's Yankee Lima 17 doing?"

"She's as strong as ever." Fred's voice was laced with pride. "We did a full maintenance check last night."

Those crew chiefs treated their aircraft like high-end racecars and took immense pride in their work. The 34s were their babies. That was fine with me, considering how our lives depended upon them.

"Good to know," I said. "Let's take care of each other out there today."

"Yes, suh." He popped a quick salute.

I smiled and popped one back.

Steve and I performed an exterior preflight check of the aircraft, then climbed inside the cockpit. It was like an oven. My flight suit was soaked before we finished our pre-start-up list.

I turned to look at Steve and got a sharp burn on my neck from the metal buckle on the seat strap. "Fuck!" I yelled. I thought to myself, *Rick, can you please try to make a mental note to remember to turn up your collar to keep the seat buckle from branding you, especially since this isn't the first time? You'd think it would only take one time not to forget. Yeah, well, whatever.* I tended to have conversations with myself from time to time.

Once through the checklist, I turned on the battery and ignited the big radial 1820. As always, we were treated to a beautiful, visceral combination of sounds and smells as the engine delivered a huge cough and a plume of acrid smoke curled from the exhaust pipes just below the cockpit. The beast awakened. Once we were up to the proper power setting, I engaged the rotor head. The blades overhead began their slow rotation, increasing in speed until the high whine combined with the roar of the engine.

As I lifted up on the collective, we struggled into the air. I applied forward pressure on the stick, and, with a slight nose-down attitude, we slid outward and upward into the heat and haze, heading north to the DMZ.

We spent the morning ferrying supplies and replacements to several LZs just south of the DMZ. At midday, we returned to Khe Sanh to grab some chow and refuel. I was the second aircraft in the flight of two 34s led by Major Styles. As the operations officer, he flew somewhat infrequently. He was a good pilot, I heard, but his desk time limited his flight time.

The protocol was for the second aircraft to follow the lead of the first aircraft, which included refueling. We never took on more than half a tank of fuel in order to limit the weight of the aircraft and help its performance.

As we began to refuel, I watched Major Styles in the aircraft in front of me and my fuel gauge at the same time. It approached half-full, and Major Styles was still taking on fuel. Alarm bells rang in my head. As my gauge continued to rise, I shouted to my crew chief over the intercom. "Fred, stop fueling NOW!"

"Yes, suh!" he shouted back.

Shit.

Major Styles had stopped fueling as well by then.

I thought about radioing him to ask, "What the fuck?"

I thought better of it. It would have been a bit public, as other aircraft share the same radio frequency. He was a major, after all, and I was just a shitty little lieutenant.

Well, I thought, *best let it pass.*

Anyway, maybe we'd be flying for a while before going into a high-altitude LZ and have a chance to burn off some fuel and lighten our load. Nope. We were ordered to take supplies to a small mountain-top LZ maybe fifteen minutes away. Great. With the supplies and extra fuel, I was so heavy I had to do a rolling takeoff just to get us airborne. Up, up, and away we went.

Approaching the LZ, I could see it sitting atop what for all practical purposes was a jungle-covered pyramid. The landing area was just big enough to set a 34 on, surrounded by a series of trenches, bunkers, and three-foot-tall concertina barbed wire. The Marines manning that shithole should have been wearing harnesses to keep from falling over the precipice on all sides.

Life on those mountaintop outposts was grim. We frequently had to fly poor grunts to the field hospital to be treated for rat bites, as all their garbage got thrown over the wire to the slopes below. Sanitation was nonexistent.

An approach to a small LZ like that while overloaded is exacting. There's zero room for error. There's no wave-off or going around for another try once you're past the fail-safe point. The approach is a glide slope and must be right on the button. If you're too high or too low, you won't have enough power to abort the approach. It's like sliding down a railing with nothing to stop you at the bottom but the ground.

We rendezvoused over the LZ. Major Styles would go first. I watched as he chose his glide slope and made his approach. All went well. The cargo was unloaded, and two Marines got on board. He put the 34 in a three-foot hover, and I could see he was struggling to maintain even that. He set the bird down and tried again, with the same result. Spending too much time in those LZs near the DMZ was a bad idea—the local North Vietnamese boys loved to lob mortar rounds at juicy targets like helicopters, and they definitely had these zones zeroed in.

The two Marines who had boarded got out of the aircraft. Major Styles again got the 34 into a hover. This time, it was more stable. He finally got enough height to creep over the rolls of concertina wire surrounding the landing pad, wobble out over the edge of the LZ, and drop down the side of the mountain to gain some airspeed.

I was talking to myself again inside my head. *Oh good, it's my turn. If it weren't for the fucking extra fuel weight, it wouldn't be such a high pucker factor. Oh, stop bitching and fly.*

I picked my approach line and guided the 34 down, coordinating the collective, power, and the cyclic stick to stay on the glide slope I'd visualized. We slowly approached the LZ, which looked like a postage stamp. About two hundred feet out, we passed the point of no return.

Then the first mortar round hit just below the LZ on the far side. I had no choice but to continue. We slid over the wire and set down with a bit of a thud. Fred was shoving ammo and boxes out as quickly as he could when the second round hit just to the left of the pad. It sent rocks and tree limbs into the zone and into the side of the 34.

I keyed the mic for my copilot. "Steve, put your hands on the controls with me in case I get hit." Copilots always had their hands near the controls when entering or leaving an LZ just in case, but I wanted his actually on them—he'd need instantaneous control if anything happened.

He nodded and complied.

"Frank, are we ready to get the fuck out of here?" I yelled at my crew chief.

"Everything's out, sir!" he yelled over the roar of the engine.

I had on full power, and we were already at top RPMs for our departure. I pulled up on the collective. We got maybe a two-foot hover, with three feet of concertina wire thirty feet in front of me. Another round hit on the left side, this time sending shrapnel through the body of the 34.

Somewhere in the past, I'd heard of a maneuver called the "Sikorsky bounce." The H-34 had two big wheel struts in the front that telescoped back into themselves, offering some spring suspension when landing. By pumping the collective up and down, a pilot could cause the helicopter to "hop" along. It wasn't in the manual or flight training, to be sure.

Looking back years later, I couldn't remember why that idea popped into my head. I don't remember if I even thought about what I was about to do. I didn't even take a moment to see if the crew had been hit by the shrapnel. I jerked the collective up into about a three-foot hover, and the RPMs immediately dropped off, approaching the low-end redline. I jammed the collective down, and the aircraft slammed into the ground and recoiled back up. At the same time, I jerked up on the collective again and punched the 34 forward all in one violent motion. I saw the RPMs drop below the redline on the gauge as we lurched over the wire.

My heart was in my throat as I punched the nose of the 34 down over the face of the cliff. The tail wheel cleared the huge roll of concertina wire by inches, just as another mortar round fell in the middle of the landing pad. My eyes were glued to the RPM gauge as we hurtled downward toward the jungle floor. Slowly, the RPMs increased as the wind rushing over the blades allowed for less resistance. About two hundred feet above the jungle floor, we were flying again. I turned south out of the valley, and we gained altitude and our breath.

"Never seen anything like that, LT," Frank's voice came over the intercom. "When did yah learn how ta do that?"

"Just now," I replied. I tried to sound calm, although I most certainly was not.

"No shit, suh, that was fuckin' sumpin' else." Frank was as amped as all of us.

"You guys okay down there?" I asked. *Shit*, I thought. I'd been so involved with the flying I'd forgotten about the hit we took.

"Yes, suh, we're good. A few holes is all."

8. *The Sikorsky Bounce*

I looked over at Steve. We stared at one another for a while. He held up five fingers—he meant he'd just used the fifth of the nine lives we all liked to think we had. I shook my head side to side.

It was quiet the rest of the way back to Khe Sanh, each of us probably reliving those tense moments. I realized how close we'd come to disaster.

We landed at Khe Sanh, took on more supplies, and spent the rest of the day ferrying them to LZs in that area. At the end of the day, we returned to Phu Bai.

As I exited the aircraft, Major Styles, bathed in sweat, his handlebar mustache at full droop, walked over to me. "Lieutenant, you and I both know I screwed up back at Khe Sanh by taking on too much fuel."

"Well, Major, it would have been better to be a little lighter, for sure, but it worked out okay. Plus, we were able to demonstrate our superb flying skills." I hoped my joke would break the tension I could see in his face.

"No, Lieutenant, it is not okay. I appreciate your attitude, but my mistake put all of us in danger. I want you to know that I'll be writing up a report on my mistake. It simply cannot go unreported. It's for the good of all the other pilots, who might make the same mistake. Taking your eye off the fuel gauge in that situation isn't acceptable." He gave me a wry smile. "By the way, maybe someday you can teach me that Sikorsky bounce." The major turned away, headed for the squadron operations shack to write his report.

As I watched his sweat-drenched back depart, I thought, *Fucking A! Good for you, Major. That's the kind of leadership I admire.*

I hoped I'd see him at the O Club that night so I could buy him a beer or two. Lieutenant Screwdriver certainly would be in fine form.

9

Flying for the ROKs

June 15 was another blistering day. We gathered early in the operations shack for our orders. Sam Saunders and I had been assigned to fly for the ROKs, the Republic of Korea. Those were the South Korean marines assigned to an area south of Da Nang. The assignment generally was a good one in that the ROKs rarely went out of their bases on operations. They had a system that made it seldom necessary. When they did go out, they made sure to kill any living thing within their area of responsibility.

Those men were ruthless. They were hard, brutal fighters, commanded by a one-star general who was almost as hard on his men as he was on the enemy. Physical beatings were common punishment for enlisted men who made any mistake. The marines generally spent the first half of the day in physical training. In the sweltering equatorial heat, they ran with small sandbags strapped to their ankles. After a few tours through the obstacle course, they'd practice hand-to-hand combat. Their fights were no-holds-barred. Most men came out looking as though they'd been in a bar fight. The dark eyes that peered out from those tan shaven heads reminded me of wolves. They were just as lethal, and just as determined. They had nothing to lose.

Our daily routine with them was usually the same. After landing, we'd make trip after trip to the Da Nang PX store. The officers would load up on all manner of electronic gear, which they'd send back home to South Korea. Once that military operation was concluded, we'd return to their base, land, shut down the aircraft, and join them for a more-than-forgettable lunch.

Afterward, we'd join them in the main building for the afternoon American movie fest. They usually showed classic westerns. An officer would escort us inside and clear a path with his swagger stick, whacking the poor enlisted ROK marines out of the way to get us the best seats. It was something to see.

9. Flying for the ROKs

Of course, every now and then the ROK marines would mount an operation outside the base. Not much ever happened—the VC were terrified of those men and rarely ventured into the area. The South Koreans hated the communists as a result of the Korean War, and took pleasure in exacting horrific revenge on those they encountered.

Sam and I set our birds down inside the ROK compound. We were ten minutes late. To our left, standing along the edge of the landing pad, was a line of officers and NCOs in descending order of rank. Once we were shut down, I looked over and watched as one by one, each officer slugged the officer next to him square in the face, knocking him to the ground. I never learned why, but I assumed it had something to do with us being late. I have no idea why they took it out on one another. The last man in line was a radioman with his radio sitting beside him. After he took his blow, he looked around, then kicked the radio as hard as he could. I couldn't believe my eyes. I thought I was watching a *Three Stooges* clip.

I keyed the mic. Sam hadn't flown for the ROKs before, and I wondered what he thought. "Did you see that shit?" I asked.

"I'd heard about these crazy bastards," he replied. "But that is more than crazy."

I wondered if I should get out of the aircraft or not.

Just then, one of the officers walked over and spoke to my crew chief, Ken. "Sir, the major here says he wants us to take him and a few others to the Da Nang PX."

Standard operation, after all.

"Sergeant, tell him to load up no more than three men to a bird." I knew we'd be loaded down with a lot of gear on the return trip.

"Will do, sir," Ken replied.

I watched the major pick his officers. We loaded everyone on and set off on the taxi ride to the Da Nang PX. By midday, we'd made two more round trips. *Hopefully, we'll be watching movies the rest of the afternoon,* I thought.

Nope. The major gave us orders to head out to an LZ and pick up some captured VC they were holding. A bad feeling began to come over me.

The ROKs had invented a surefire way to interrogate any hapless VC they captured. They'd round up three or four suspects and fly them back to the base. On the way, they'd toss out one or two. Whoever was left would become incredibly conversational.

Pop a Smoke

I tuned to the radio frequency for the ROK base and asked to speak to the major we were working with. As a pilot in the U.S. military, we had ultimate authority in our aircraft. We could, if we felt it was warranted, override any request by a higher-ranking officer in our aircraft. We could even tell a general no, if necessary. Eventually, the major got on the wire.

"Major," I said, "I want your personal assurance that none of your men will toss anyone out of either of these aircraft on our way back."

"Don't worry, Lieutenant," came the fake assured response. "You have my word."

I could almost feel his grin. *That was too easy*, I thought. Not good.

Once airborne, I keyed the mic to my crew chief. "Sergeant, when we land in the LZ, I want you to take out your sidearm and hold it in your hand. If any of those fucking ROKs even looks like he's going to toss out one of those VC, I want you to point that .45 directly at his head and shake your head side to side indicating 'no.' Do you understand?"

My copilot, Todd Hansen, slowly turned his head and stared at me.

There was a long pause, and then Ken's slow, drawn-out reply. "Well, sir, I understand. But ... you don't actually expect me to shoot him, do you?"

"No, but you need to make him believe you will. If necessary, you fire a round out the door and then point the weapon back in his face. Do you understand?"

After another long pause, he replied. "Yes, sir."

I had two ROKs in my aircraft and two loaded up in Sam's. It was only a twenty-minute hop out to the LZ. I tuned in the LZ frequency and contacted the ground unit. "This is Yankee Lima 33. We are inbound for a prisoner pickup. Pop smoke, please."

There was no response, but I could see yellow smoke rising straight up in the windless air. *I hate flying for these cowboys*, I thought. *They play by their own rules, and I have little choice but to go along for the ride.* Certainly U.S. command knew the score, but there was little they could or would do either. The ROKs served a purpose. They filled a void.

There seemed to be no threat of enemy fire on the LZ, which was more than appreciated. Sam and I landed in formation a few meters apart. Two ROKs approached my aircraft with three VC, bound and blindfolded. Even the small ROK marines looked big next to those small humans in black pajamas. I'm sure they were terrified and feared the worst.

9. Flying for the ROKs

All I could think was, *I need to get them back to the base in one piece. I don't want any shit going down on my watch. After that, it's up to the ROKs and God, though I'm sure they don't believe in God.*

The two ROKs in Sam's 34 climbed out. Three others climbed in.

I keyed the mic. "You ready, Sam?"

"Ready, Rick."

I keyed the mic again. "Sergeant, do you have your .45 out?"

"Yes, sir, I do." He sounded calm.

"Do the ROKs see it in your hand?"

"Yes, sir, they do."

"I want you to raise the pistol to the ceiling and chamber a round and make sure they see you do it." I waited. I knew I was asking a lot of Ken, but it had to be done.

"Round chambered, sir."

"This is Yankee Lima 33, departing stage right," I called over the radio.

"Roger that, 33," Sam replied.

We climbed to about 2,500 feet and turned back toward the ROK base. As we leveled off, my crew chief keyed the mic.

"Something is going on, sir. They just took the blindfolds off the three VC and moved one toward the door."

"Sergeant, I want you to fire a round out the door, and then point that fucking .45 right in one of their faces. Then slowly move your head side to side. Do it now." I could hear the .45 go off. Then there was silence except for the roar of the engine and thump of the rotor blades.

"Sir, he just threw out one of the VC, and he's just smiling at me. I think he knows I can't shoot him, or I won't. What should I do?"

I thought for a moment. "Sergeant, if he moves that other VC to the door, I want you to point your weapon at the third prisoner. Tell him you will shoot that prisoner if he throws out the second one. Make him understand. Maybe he thinks you won't shoot him, but if he thinks you'll shoot the last VC, he'll understand he'll have no one left to interrogate. You can't shoot a prisoner, but this is our last chance to bluff him."

"Yes, sir." There was a long silence. "I used some sign language. I'm not sure the ROK understands, but at least he hasn't moved anyone else to the door."

"Okay. We're only a few minutes from base. Don't let your guard down, Sergeant. Keep that .45 pointed at someone."

Both 34s landed in formation on the pad in front of the main building. The ROKs in Sam's bird departed first. Then the two ROKs in my bird departed with the two VC. I noticed they'd been blindfolded again.

The ROK sergeant led them a few yards, then turned and stared at me. With a grin, he gave me a salute. I put my arm out the window and shot him the bird. I held it until he turned away. Then I cranked on the power and put the 34 into a ten-foot hover and held it there in order to blow as much sand and dirt on that bastard as I could. They all disappeared in a cloud of dust as they walked toward their operations building.

I keyed my mic. "Sam, we're out of here."

"Roger that, Rick. Right behind you."

We'd not been officially released by the ROKs, but I'd had enough of those assholes. If they wanted to file a complaint, they could have at it. I was pretty sure my CO would back me up under the circumstances.

Once we returned to Phu Bai, I made sure to tell Ken, my crew chief, what a good job he'd done in a tough situation. Then I marched into the operations shack and asked for the CO.

"Colonel Schmidt," the duty sergeant said, "is on leave in Japan."

How many leaves does this guy get anyway? I thought. *Jesus.*

"The XO is in," the sergeant offered. "You can talk to him if you want, sir."

The XO, Colonel Burns, was a straight-up guy, and I preferred him anyway. "Fine," I replied. The duty sergeant checked with the XO, then escorted me into his office.

I marched up to his desk and snapped a smart salute. I was pretty heated, and I told him everything that had happened.

He listened quietly until I'd finished. "Lieutenant, write your report, and I'll send it up the chain. But both you and I know nothing will come of it. The ROKs are a separate military, and we have no control over how they operate—even if they did violate the Geneva Convention by tossing that VC out of your bird. Still, we need to follow our own protocol, so give me your report by the end of the day. I know it sucks, but there it is. Dismissed."

That was the end of our discussion. I saluted, turned on my heel, and exited the office. I made a quick trip to the O Club for two doubles. Then it was back to my hooch to write my report.

A lot of bad shit goes down in war. If I'd been a ground-pounder,

I might not have been so worked up, but goddamn it, that was my aircraft, and I wasn't able to stop the cold-blooded murder of a bound-and-gagged prisoner. They'd stained me and my aircraft. Somehow, I felt responsible, and no logic or excuse would ever be enough for me to absolve myself. It was a deep wound.

10

Incoming or Outgoing?

The midsummer heat in Vietnam is nearly unbearable, especially when there's no breeze. Some days, we didn't fly, and were left to amuse ourselves as best we could. With all the sand around, we tried to pretend we were at the beach, but it was a lost cause without an ocean. Plus, the sun was unrelenting. Eight lily-white bodies sprawled on cots outside a hooch wasn't a pretty sight. We looked like an ad for Solarcaine.

Playing poker during the day inside the hooch was just as miserable. It was like being inside an oven—in fact, we'd nicknamed our hooch Westing House. The sun turned the tin roof into a frying pan. Some days, I'd just go stand in the tepid water of the shower. The water supply was limited, so that was always a short reprieve. No-fly days were long and boring, but on the other hand, some flying days cost one of our nine lives.

Phu Bai also was home to an artillery unit, which frequently was engaged in sending gift packages to the enemy at the request of various units on the front lines. The outgoing rounds made a deep *whump* sound each time they passed overhead. Some days, it lasted an hour or more.

Phu Bai also was in range of occasional rocket attacks launched by the NVA and the Viet Cong. Their weapon of choice was a 122 mm rocket. The rocket itself was just over eight feet long, weighed just over one hundred pounds, and had a range of about seven miles. The rockets were produced by Russia and supplied to the North Vietnamese beginning in 1967. The rockets could be fired from rocket-launching trucks, but more commonly came from improvised bamboo firing stakes. These were simply two pieces of bamboo lashed together to form a big X. The rocket was placed at an angle in the top of the X and pointed toward the target. They weren't very accurate, but enough of them fired at once could cause considerable damage.

10. Incoming or Outgoing?

The rockets were transported by trucks, or on the backs of Vietnamese soldiers. They humped those babies all the way down the Ho Chi Minh Trail through Laos and Cambodia. It was an arduous trek along roads, trails, and paths, and it lasted perhaps a month. Making it even more difficult, the Ho Chi Minh Trail was subject to constant bombing from U.S. forces.

The lucky North Vietnamese soldier would make the month-long journey with the eight-foot-long, one-hundred-pound rocket on his back. If he survived the bombings and the constant threat of death by malaria or dysentery, he'd have the pleasure of firing that rocket. He'd then turn around, go back to North Vietnam, and do it all again. Nice life.

Rocket attacks at Phu Bai were fairly common. The disconcerting thing was that when one landed, it landed with a *whump*. Distinguishing the outgoing *whump* of an artillery round and the incoming *whump* of a 122 mm rocket was a skill that took months to develop.

However, the boys in Westing House had a secret weapon—Art Fanning. Art had been in-country longer than the rest of us and had the keenly honed ability to determine one *whump* from the other. In fact, Art could almost tell one was coming before it arrived.

If Art seemed a little nervous at times, we all felt nervous. When we were treated to a bad *whump*, we all hauled ass out of the hooch and into the bunker next to us. There was a bunker between each hooch. All the bunkers had a front and rear entry and were typically a low-roofed rectangle constructed of sandbags and fifty-gallon steel drums filled with sand. All eight of us could stuff ourselves in there, but just barely. Sitting there as the rockets landed, you felt helpless. All you could do was listen for the impact and judge its proximity by how much noise it made. We all hoped we wouldn't receive a direct hit. The sandbag bunker wouldn't withstand it.

The NVA weren't stupid. They knew the outgoing artillery rounds sounded just like the incoming rocket rounds. So they'd frequently wait to fire their rockets until we began an outgoing artillery barrage, thereby disguising their assault.

One particular evening, we were all sitting around playing poker, and the hooch shook with a *whump*. All eyes instantaneously and in complete synchronization turned toward Art. No reaction. The game continued. *Whump! Whump! Whump!* All eyes on Art. A slight pause.... *Whump!* Art bolted for the door, with all of us right behind him.

Art Fanning (left) and me outside the hooch, June 1969 (author's collection).

Whump! Whump! The base siren sounded, indicating we were under a rocket attack. No shit.

They ought to wire Art to that siren. It would go off sooner.

We crouched in the dank air of the bunker. Only a sliver of light from the front and rear entries penetrated the darkness. The thin shaft vibrated as dust and sand rained from the roof.

This feels a bit too much like a tomb, I thought.

The next *whump* was bone-shattering. The rocket had landed next to the bunker. I couldn't see two feet in front of me.

Someone yelled, "Everyone okay?"

A lot of expletives followed, but other than some fillings being jarred loose, it seemed everyone was in one piece.

10. Incoming or Outgoing?

I suspected the hooch next to us had taken a direct hit. That was concerning because some guys seemed to prefer rolling under their racks during a rocket attack rather than taking the trouble to go to the bunker. There was a major in the hooch next door who made a habit of it.

Pete Peterson was crouched next to me. I elbowed him. "Come on. We need to check if anyone's hurt."

I was banking on the logic that the next round wouldn't be that close, if it did come in. We low-crawled out the rear of the bunker. I peeked around the corner and saw nothing left of the hooch next door. We waited a few minutes. No more rounds exploded.

I stood up and walked among the debris of the hooch. The rocket had gone right through the roof, straight through the major's bunk, and penetrated the concrete slab of the hooch. The first two feet of what was left of the rocket was still sticking out of the slab. I stared at it. I could read the lettering on its side: *CCCP 122 MM.*

Knowing that Russia was supplying arms to the North Vietnamese was one thing; seeing those letters on a rocket that almost killed all of us was another. I can still see those letters today as clearly as I saw them then.

The rest of the guys had emerged from the bunker just as the all-clear siren sounded. They, too, milled around what was left of the hooch.

"Where's the major?" someone asked.

I shrugged. "Wherever he is, he's one lucky sonofabitch he wasn't in the hooch. He would have been skewered by that 122."

Just then the major came walking down the path between the hooches. He looked a bit disheveled. As he neared, we could see he was covered in … shit. He'd been sitting on the two-holers down the path when a rocket had landed nearby. It blew the two-holer over with him in it.

Before I could think, I said, "Holy shit, Major, are you okay?" As soon as the words left my mouth, I cringed. *Try to think!* I told myself. *Don't let your mouth get in front of your brain, you idiot!*

"You're going to regret that remark, you son of a bitch," the major stammered.

"Sorry, sir. I didn't mean it that way."

The rest of the guys were doing everything they could to stifle their laughter. There was a lot of throat clearing and coughing around us.

"Get the fuck out of my way," the major barked as he pushed past us and on toward the showers. No worries there. The smell alone would have parted the Red Sea.

Casualties weren't always due to enemy fire. Some were caused by flying accidents or mechanical failures. Don Bosberry, a guy who'd been in my squadron back in Santa Ana, had died a week earlier. The H-46 he was flying lost its front rotor at three thousand feet when its retaining nut came loose. The recovery team found the pilots' bodies a mile from the wreckage. The vibration of the helicopter with only one rotor blade going was so devastating that they were catapulted through the front of the cockpit still strapped in their seats. Don had been one of those pilots who transitioned from the H-34 into the H-46 prior to our deployment.

Several weeks prior to that, there had been another accident. Toby Hicks, flying a Huey, was in a midair collision over the runway at Marble Mountain, just outside of Da Nang. The two Hueys were in formation and were to make a right-hand break over the runway to set up their approach. Word was that someone broke the wrong way. Both crews perished in a fireball.

By then, I was in my sixth month in Vietnam. I hadn't started what was called a "short-timer's calendar" because I was anything but. The end of my tour still seemed so far away that all a calendar would have done was depress me or add to the nagging belief that I wasn't going to make it through.

Of the 11,827 helicopters put into service in Vietnam, 5,086 were destroyed. Some 2,165 pilots and 2,712 crewmembers lost their lives. The statistics are much worse for an infantry lieutenant, whose life expectancy in the Marine Corps in Vietnam averaged two months. In the Army, it was closer to days. A lieutenant leading his men on a helicopter assault into a hot LZ was *always* the first one out, making him the first-choice target of the enemy.

I had seven months remaining. It might as well have been seventy.

11

Hill 818

It was a Tuesday morning in September, and still hotter than hell. The squadron pilots were waiting, as usual, in the ready room for assignments. I was assigned Dave Evans as my copilot, a man I'd flown with several times already.

"Good to be flying together again, Rick," Dave said as we awaited orders. Dave was senior in time to me, but as I was the last pilot assigned to HMM-362, there were no more junior pilots. So, as usual, the squadron rotated pilot and copilot duties to keep everyone sharp.

"Good indeed," I replied. "It's been a while. How's that wife and baby of yours?" Dave's wife had given birth to a girl a few weeks before we shipped out.

"They're both great." Dave sported a big grin. He looked like a movie star with his big, square, chiseled face, brilliant blue eyes, and a set of white teeth that looked like an ad for Colgate. He reminded me of Charlton Heston around *Ben Hur* time. "Take a look," he said and pulled a picture from the pocket of his flight suit. His wife, Becky, who looked like a movie star herself, was holding a little blond-haired, blue-eyed girl with the same grin as Dave.

"She definitely has your smile," I said, returning the photo. "She's beautiful. They both are. You're a lucky man. I bet you can't wait to get home. What's your little girl's name?"

"Julie," he replied, staring at the picture. "It was my mother-in-law's name." After a long moment, he returned the picture to his pocket. His smile faded, and his brow furrowed as he looked across the table at me. "Did you hear about Simpson and Blankenship?"

The squadron had been flying a lot. Some missions were routine, and some not so much. Pilots hung out with one another, even some from different squadrons, especially if we'd gone through Quantico or Pensacola together. Two of those guys were Steve Simpson and Ron Blankenship, who were flying the big H-53s with HMH-463.

Steve and his copilot, Ron, were returning from a recon extraction mission on the coast just north of the DMZ when they'd encountered heavy clouds and fog. Before they could get clear, they flew face-first into one of the many mountains in the area. Two pilots, two crew members, and four recon Marines.

"Yeah, I heard." I sighed. "I guess you heard about Robinson and Skeeter too."

Todd Robinson and his copilot, Skeeter Dubois, from our squadron, HMM-362, had been shot down near the Laotian border while attempting to extract a recon team. Two pilots, two crewmembers, and four recon Marines. The second aircraft circling overhead reported they'd picked up the recon team in a valley and were almost out when they were hit by a .50 cal.

Recon inserts and extracts were the most hazardous assignments. The Force Recon Marines were the toughest, most versatile, resilient, and fearsome warriors on the planet—because they had to be. Dropping into enemy-infested areas to gather intelligence without being detected, then getting out alive, was no small feat. It generally didn't go without incident. Maybe they could get in without being detected but getting out was a lot more difficult. Generally, they were supposed to avoid contact, but if they did become engaged with the enemy, God help those on the receiving end.

In 1967, Major James Steele of the III Marine Amphibious Force Intelligence section began comparing statistics between Force Recon and regular Marine units. The results were startling. Steele determined that the kill ratio for regular Marines was seven enemies killed for every Marine lost. For Force Recon, the ratio was thirty-four enemies killed for every Force Recon Marine lost. In the category of enemy contact, he revealed that with regular Marine units, the enemy initiated contact 80 percent of the time. With Force Recon, in an astonishing 95 percent of the incidents, it was Force Recon that initiated the contact.

Most recon inserts and extracts took place in the mountainous areas of western Vietnam. That was where the concentrations of NVA were the highest, with so many people coming down the Ho Chi Minh Trail to infiltrate South Vietnam. The job of the recon Marines was to find them and report back with information on strength and disposition, etc. The idea was to get in and out without being detected. However, the units never passed up the opportunity to set up an ambush when they thought they had the advantage.

Let's face it, an NVA force concentrated in an area usually heard us coming. They might not see where we were, or where we dropped off these poor bastards, but they knew it was nearby. That started an NVA hunt to find them. It was a matter of who found whom.

The Marine recon team's mission was to try to locate perhaps a company or battalion of NVA, and then determine their strength, location, and any other pertinent intelligence. Then they had to get back out undetected and report what they'd found to headquarters. It was unbelievably dangerous and difficult work.

Our orders came down. Dave and I were assigned to good old Yankee Lima 13. Steve Bradbury and his copilot, Warren Franks, were assigned to Yankee Lima 22. Our mission was to ferry two recon teams to a firebase on Hill 818, which was tucked into the northwest corner of Vietnam, just south of the DMZ and just east of the Laotian border and the Ho Chi Minh Trail. Hill 818 had been the scene of some intense fighting during the siege of Khe Sanh.

At least we'll be landing at a real landing zone at a firebase rather than out in the boonies somewhere, I thought.

The two recon teams were to depart the next day from the firebase into the mountainous areas to the west.

Dave and I gathered our gear and headed to the aircraft. As usual, I carried my .45 and my old pal the M79 grenade launcher. Dave also had a .45 as well as an M16. We marched out to the aircraft, where the crew chief, Stacy Brinkman, and gunner, Keg Johnson, waited.

"Gentlemen," I said, offering a salute. "How the hell are you?"

They both smiled and saluted back.

"Still standing, LT," Stacy replied. "How are you?"

"Glad to be with you boys again. How's Yankee Lima 13?"

"Strong as she can be, sir. We put her through a full maintenance check two days ago. Full checkup again last night."

Those crew chiefs loved their aircraft, and we all certainly depended on their ability to get the most out of them. That being said, the old 34 was just that. Old. Nonetheless, those of us who flew them loved them. We referred to them as the "Timex of helicopters." They could take a licking and keep on ticking.

Dave and I conducted our walk-around preflight check, then climbed into the cockpit. I stashed my M79 behind my seat, sat down, strapped in, and swung my sidearm holster with my .45 around to my left side.

Dave and I went through the preflight checklist together. I turned on the ignition and cranked up the big 1820 radial engine. To this day, I can still hear the big engine cough and catch its breath as it came to life in a roar of power. Dave and I scanned the gauges to ensure all was well and waited for the RPMs to come up to speed. The 34 began rocking back and forth a bit as if asking, *When are you going to engage the fan?*

Soon, my friend, soon, I thought.

When all the gauges and temps read as they should, I engaged the rotor head. Slowly, the rotor blades began their clockwise rotation. The collective was all the way down, giving the blades a flat pitch as they increased in speed. Once up to speed, the old gal was ready to fly and waiting for the command.

I looked over at Dave, who nodded and gave me a thumbs-up. I keyed the mic. "Stacy, you and Keg set down there?"

"Yessir, LT."

I radioed to Steve Bradbury. "Yankee Lima 22, this is Yankee Lima 13. Steve, I'd like to do a runway rolling formation takeoff, just to show off a bit, if you like." Normally we'd just put the birds in a hover and depart, but I wanted to mix things up a bit.

"Sounds good, 13," Steve replied.

I checked to ensure we were on tower frequency, then keyed the mic. "Phu Bai tower, this is Yankee Lima 13 with a flight of two. Permission for a rolling takeoff."

"Roger, Yankee Lima 13. Cleared for takeoff."

With Yankee Lima 22 slightly behind my right side, we taxied in formation to the runway and positioned our aircraft. I keyed the mic to the tower. "Yankee Lima 13 and 22 rolling."

"Roger, 13."

I increased the power, raised the collective, and pushed the cyclic forward. We began rolling forward, both aircraft in unison down the runway. I gave it a little more power and raised the collective a bit more with more forward cyclic, and the tail wheel left the ground. Nose down, we accelerated forward. Adding more power and lifting up more on the collective, we accelerated more, then the front wheels left the runway, and we were airborne. Smooth as silk. Still in perfect formation, we headed west to pick up our passengers.

Once again, we looked down at the checkerboard of rice paddies glistening in the sun and the lush jungle in the distance. And once again, I was struck by the natural beauty of what seemed such a serene and peaceful landscape. Just below, a family of five was bent at the waist, planting a new crop of rice plants in the paddy next to their thatched-roof hut. Smoke rose from the cooking pots of the village nearby as a young girl herded a flock of geese through the square. A light breeze ruffled some brightly colored banners attached to a church in the middle of the village.

What a dichotomy. Somewhere down there was the enemy, ready to unleash deadly violence on any U.S. or South Vietnamese forces encountered. Caught between those combatants were the Vietnamese civilians, who would pay the highest price. Harassed and threatened by the Viet Cong, who constantly took their food and provisions, and conscripted their young men into their ranks, the villagers lived in fear. Not only of the VC, but also of the Americans who patrolled the villages and dealt out their own justice if they found any reason to think the villagers had aided the enemy. They were damned if they did and damned if they didn't.

Once airborne, we turned north to a small base just west of Quang Tri to pick up two four-man units of recon Marines. The base was nothing but a few ramshackle buildings and sandbag bunkers surrounded by concertina wire situated out in the open just west of Highway 1. Sparse and severe, just like the men who inhabited it.

As we approached the installation, Dave turned the radio to the base frequency. The call sign was Iron Fist.

I keyed the mic. "Iron Fist, this is Yankee Lima 13 and Yankee Lima 22, inbound for a pickup."

"Roger that, Yankee Lima 13. Cleared to land."

I radioed to Yankee Lima 22. "Steve, looks like there's enough room for both of us, so let's go in together."

"Roger, Rick. I'm behind and on your right."

We made a standard formation landing into the zone, sending up red dust swirling into a cloud so thick it obliterated everything. We sat there, waiting for the visibility to improve, hoping our idling rotor heads would minimize the dust storm. No such luck. The morning sun straining through the dust turned the LZ into a sea of swirling orange.

Like the four horsemen of the apocalypse with the sun behind them, the silhouettes of the first recon team emerged from the dust storm, headed in our direction. Dressed in the typical recon camo attire, they were heavily armed, and their faces were painted green and black. They looked as fearsome as I knew they were. Warrior breed. The second four-man team moved out of the swirling cloud and headed toward Yankee Lima 22.

Each 34 was loaded and ready to depart in minutes. I keyed the intercom. "Stacy, you ready down there?"

"Ready, LT."

I keyed the radio to Yankee Lima 22. "Steve, you ready?"

"Ready, Rick."

I had Dave switch to the base frequency and keyed the mic again. "Iron Fist, Yankee Lima 13 and Yankee Lima 22 are departing."

"Roger, 13. Good luck."

Good luck? I thought. *Does he know something I don't?* He probably did. But I guess any recon mission needed all the luck it could get.

Our 34s lifted off, and once again we headed west into the mountains and equatorial jungles of Vietnam. Within thirty minutes, we were approaching Hill 818, our drop-off point.

I had Dave switch to the LZ frequency so I could check in. "LZ Storm, this is Yankee Lima 13 and 22 approaching with troops."

"Roger, Yankee Lima 13," came the reply. "Be aware we have been in intermediate contact today."

Great, I thought. "Roger, Storm," I called back. *It's all part of the job, and the risk involved*, I told myself. *It's probably why we get paid so much, right?* I keyed the mic to Steve. "Yankee Lima 22, I will go in first. If all goes well, begin your approach as soon as I'm coming out."

"Roger, 13."

I keyed the intercom to the crew below. "Stacy, you and Keg be alert and ready to return any fire we get. Keg, clear that M60."

"Roger, sir," Stacy replied.

Keg cranked out two short bursts from the M60 as we began circling the LZ.

I keyed the mic to the zone. "Storm, pop a smoke, please."

"Roger, popping smoke."

A column of orange smoke rose from the LZ. It moved slightly to the southeast, giving Steve and me vital information about the wind direction. Obviously, the sound of our helicopters and the smoke rising from the zone announced our arrival to the enemy, but there wasn't any other option.

I keyed the mic. "Steve, I'm going to head back east again. Get down to the deck and make a pop-up approach into the zone. You wait until I'm out before you begin your descent."

"Roger that, 13."

We both knew this type of an approach, rather than a high-altitude glide slope, would give us more cover time and minimize our exposure to enemy fire. My hope was that the enemy wasn't concentrated in that valley, but one of the others situated around the hilltop.

I keyed the intercom to Dave. "Keep your hands on the controls with me as we get close to the LZ."

"Roger, Rick."

We were at three thousand feet at the head of the valley. I dropped the collective and punched the nose over, and we began our descent. Our airspeed increased, and we were going as fast as a fully loaded 34 could go as we skimmed above the treetops back west to the LZ.

The hilltop zone soon appeared ahead and above us, the orange smoke still swirling around the firebase. Squeezing every bit of speed possible out of Yankee Lima 13, I raised the collective and the nose at the same time. I was using all the inertia I could to pop up the side of the mountain and hopefully make a pinpoint landing inside the perimeter.

The 34 had just cleared the level of the hilltop when we were raked by machine-gun fire. The first rounds took out most of the cockpit windshield and stitched the fuselage down along the side to the tail rotor. The 34 shuddered like a heavyweight boxer taking a punch.

We still weren't over the zone, and the 34 began to spin to the right. I knew instantly that the ground fire had hit the tail rotor and we were going down. I tried to slide us over the zone as we continued in a snapping spiral. If we crashed in the zone, we might survive. If we missed the zone and hit the hillside … well, we'd just somersault downward.

The engine was over-speeding, trying to carry the enormous torque the fuselage was under. The scream of the engine was deafening, and ground fire still peppered the aircraft.

I jammed the collective down and pushed the cyclic hard to the right as we came around for the second time. We slammed into the perimeter wire and rolled onto our side. The rotor blades were thrashing the ground, and the 34 was coming apart. Pieces of broken blades crashed through the cockpit. All I could see was smoke and dust. I reached up and threw the emergency handle to stop the rotor head from its rotation. I could smell fuel. The last of the death throes of Yankee Lima 13 ceased, and for a moment there was an eerie silence. I could hear a lot of gunfire, which I hoped was the Marines at the LZ unleashing on the enemy.

We were lying on our left side. I looked down at Dave. He was slumped in his seat with what looked like a shard of rotor blade sticking from his neck, his flight suit bathed in blood. My adrenaline was at full throttle and my heart sank. He looked dead. I hoped I was wrong.

I couldn't hear anything. My mind snapped back to my crash in Santa Ana. I unstrapped and climbed up through the cockpit door above me. All I could think of was the crew and the recon boys in the belly. My fear was fire. As I mentioned, the body of an H-34 was made of magnesium alloy, and it burned hot and fast. The whole aircraft could be reduced to a melted metal hulk in minutes. If the men inside were trapped, they'd never survive a fire.

Since we were on our left side, the cargo door on the right side was facing upward, offering a means of escape. I pulled myself out of the cockpit and slid down the side of the fuselage, crumpling to the ground. Gunfire still rang out all around me. I needed help to get Dave and the crew out.

The door of the 34 was about three feet above me. From where I stood, I couldn't see inside. "Stacy! Keg! Are you in there? Are you okay?"

There was no response. I was shaking with shock and emotion.

A Marine came running from my left, firing as he ran. Once behind the 34, he hunkered down with me. "Are you okay?"

"Yeah, I'm fine. We need to get these men out before it catches fire. My copilot is badly hurt and still strapped into the cockpit."

The Marine propped his M16 against the side of the aircraft and, without a moment of hesitation, hauled himself up onto the landing gear. He peered inside the cockpit and then the belly of the 34. Then he reached inside and hauled out Stacy, who was bleeding from the head and legs. The Marine held him by one arm and lowered him gently to the ground.

Stacy was alert, but obviously in bad shape.

"Are you okay?" I shouted. "Are you hit?"

"I'm hit in the legs. Get the others out. They need help."

The Marine on the side of the helicopter continued his efforts to get the men out, even though he remained exposed to enemy fire. Shots from below peppered all around him as he pulled out Keg. He'd been shot in the back and was in bad shape. Out of nowhere, two corpsmen appeared and began treating him and Stacy.

The Marine on the helicopter next helped each of the recon Marines out. He shouted something to them, then ducked into the cockpit. They waited, still exposed to the enemy fire, until the Marine reappeared. He was shepherding Dave's limp body, and hoisted him up to the recon Marines, who lowered him down. One of the corpsmen rushed over to treat Dave.

The four-man recon team then split up, and two men went to each end of the sideways 34. Using the helicopter as cover, they began throwing grenades and lighting up the hillside with automatic fire.

The whole event lasted only minutes but seemed nearly endless to me. I moved over toward Dave and looked at the corpsman working on him.

He shook his head. Dave was dead.

I felt furious and heartsick. My copilot was dead. Both my crew were wounded. I should be dead. Should I have done something different?

Dave would never again see the smiles of his wife and daughter, and they'd never see his. I reached down and took the picture of his wife and baby from his flight suit pocket. I'd make sure it got back to them.

To this day, I carry the guilt, deserved or not, for Dave's death. There's no logical reason to still feel it, but it's seared inside of me. Logic isn't part of the equation. Even writing about that day still causes it to rush from the darkness like a ghost.

I wanted to grab a weapon, any weapon, charge down the hill, and kill anyone I could find. I needed to take out my rage on someone. The M16 that that brave Marine had given me before he climbed in the 34 was still propped against the side of the chopper. I grabbed it and stormed toward the front of the aircraft.

The Marine ran up behind me and wrenched the weapon from my hands. "It's okay, Lieutenant!" he shouted. "We'll make them pay, believe me."

I breathed deeply and realized the gunfire had stopped. I took off my helmet and walked over to Stacy and Keg. The corpsmen continued working on them. One looked up and nodded at me. "They'll be fine, sir. They'll recover."

I knelt down next to my men and put my hand on their shoulders, one by one. "I'm sorry, men. So damn sorry."

Stacy lifted himself up on one elbow. "We're okay, LT. You did good. We could have been at the bottom of the mountain if you weren't such a good pilot. I don't know how you got us into the zone, but it saved our lives."

Later, I'd remember the crash in Santa Ana again and realize he was right. If I hadn't had that prior crash experience, I never would have reacted quickly enough to make it to the zone.

Keg looked up at me. His flak jacket had slowed down the round he took to the back. He was in a lot of pain, but knew he'd survive. "LT, if a door gunner goes home without a scratch, he's not worth his salt. I'll be fine. We'll fly with you anytime and hope we get that chance."

I tried to hold back my emotions. I didn't know what to say. "Me too," I managed. I turned and walked away so they couldn't see the tears welling in my eyes. I saw the Marine who'd risked his life to help us. "Corporal, where's your command bunker?"

He pointed to a low-slung bunker a few meters away.

"What's your name, son?"

"Reynolds, sir."

"You are one brave son of a bitch, Corporal. I won't forget what you did."

He smiled and winked, then turned and headed back to the perimeter wire.

I ran over to the command bunker and found the CO, Major Jenkins.

Jenkins stared at me. "You okay, Lieutenant?"

"Yes, sir. I'm fine, but my copilot is dead, and both my crewmen are wounded. I'd like to get them out of here as soon as possible."

"Your second bird wants to come in to drop off the recon boys and take you out. Can't say for sure he won't run into the same shit you did."

"Major, I sure would like to get some air support to hose down the area while we try to get these men out."

"Let me see what I can do."

"Also, I need to get on your radio and talk to my wingman."

The major nodded and pointed at the radioman seated at a desk on the other side of the cramped bunker.

"Sergeant," I said, "can you raise Yankee Lima 22 for me?"

He nodded and barked into his handset. "Yankee Lima 22, this is Ironfist. Over."

"Ironfist, this is Yankee Lima 22."

I took the mic. I tried to sound calm. "Steve, this is Rick. Dave is dead, and Stacy and Keg are wounded. The major is going to try to

116

arrange some air cover. Hoping you can exchange your cargo for mine if you're willing."

The reply was instantaneous. "Yankee Lima 22 will be coming in, with or without air cover. Keep me posted on which it will be. Hang in there, pal. We're coming either way."

"Roger, 22," was all I could muster.

The major was on the phone next. Within minutes, he'd arranged for air cover. "We've got two Cobra gunships on their way. They'll coordinate with your wingman on the operation. You can keep track on this frequency."

"Thank you, Major."

"I'm sorry about your copilot, Lieutenant."

"Yeah." I looked away.

Soon the airwaves filled with chatter as the Cobra gunships arrived on station and coordinated with Steve in Yankee Lima 22. The plan was typical for getting in and out of a hot LZ: the two gunships would make separate runs, unloading rocket and machine-gun fire into the enemy positions, which would be marked by smoke grenades launched from the firebase. Essentially, they'd be making a synchronized figure eight pattern so that one Cobra was always firing as Yankee Lima 22 made its approach, landing, and departure.

Everything was out of my hands then. I went back outside and explained the plan to the corpsmen. They got Stacy and Keg on stretchers. Dave's body was already on a stretcher in a black bag. That sight will never leave me. I sat down next to him and waited.

Within minutes, I could hear Yankee Lima 22 approaching. Next came the fusillade of firepower from the first Cobra as it poured rocket and machine-gun fire into the terrain below. There was a secondary explosion below—some of his rounds must have found an enemy ammo site. He pulled up from his run as the second Cobra screamed downward, unleashing the next torrent of firepower. Just then, Yankee Lima 22 popped up from below, transitioned into a hover, and slid over the wire onto the LZ. Four recon Marines jumped out and moved to cover.

The two corpsmen and four other Marines carried the three stretchers to Yankee Lima 22. I was right behind. We loaded in seconds. I saw Steve's crew chief speak into the mic. Steve pulled on full power, and we struggled into a four-foot hover. Slowly, we slid over the perimeter wire and dropped over the edge, heading downward to gain airspeed.

We were on the backside of the firebase and hopefully out of the enemy's line of fire. Both Cobras continued their cover fire as we gained airspeed and altitude, heading to the first medical base we could find.

It was a somber flight. Steve's crew chief attended to Stacy and Keg, trying to make them comfortable. I sat beside Dave's body, the events of the preceding hour spinning in my head. My emotions ping-ponged between feeling lucky to be alive and the deep sadness of Dave's death.

We landed at a field hospital near Phu Bai. The waiting medical staff unloaded Stacy and Keg. I jumped out and put my hands on Stacy's and Keg's shoulders for a moment before the medical staff carried them away. The two men who unloaded Dave's body paused beside me, and I stood there with my hand on him. I said a short, silent prayer, then gave him a salute and climbed back onto Yankee Lima 22.

Once back at Phu Bai, I went to the operations shack to make my report. I was emotionally and physically exhausted. The word of our ordeal already had spread through the squadron.

On my way to the office, several pilots I passed gave me a quick pat on the shoulder and said, "Glad you're back, Rick."

I just nodded and tried to smile. I felt like pure shit.

Inside the operations shack, I found the XO, Major Stephens, and the operations officer, Major Styles, waiting.

"We're sorry about Dave, Lieutenant," Major Stephens said. "But we're glad you and the crew made it back. Lieutenant Bradbury said you did a hell of a job just getting your bird into the zone. Good job, Rick."

"Thank you, Major, but I don't feel too good about much right now. Is it okay if I take some time and get my report to you later today?"

"Take as much time as you need. You're off the rotation for a couple of days. No argument."

"Sir, there was one Marine at the firebase who risked his life continually under enemy fire to get us all out of that bird. I want to write him up for a commendation."

"Write it up separately," Major Stephens said. "Then submit it with your incident report. Now get some rest."

I saluted, turned, and left the shack. Back in my hooch, a few mates greeted me with words of consolation and support, then bugged out, giving me the space they knew I needed.

11. Hill 818

I collapsed on my cot and stared at the ceiling, trying to clear my head of all that had happened. At some point, I slipped into a restless sleep. I awoke still in my flight suit, bathed in sweat. It was dark. I looked at my watch. It was 9:00 p.m. I got up and headed to the showers and then the O Club to get as drunk as I could.

12

The Twilight Zone

The days off after the mission to Hill 818 gave me time to think about myself, the war, and what we were doing. Looking back, I must admit I had no idea about the opposition to the war at home. We had no TV, and our only source of information was letters from family and friends. No one ever mentioned the protests. We lived in the day-to-day bubble of flying. I'd find out soon enough, however, and the fallout would remain with me for the rest of my life.

During those three days of rest, I thought again about my survival chances given the intensity of our flying. Other thoughts began to creep into my head. On some missions, I'd fly with pilots who were back for their second tour, and they shared how we were flying into the same zones and doing the same work as they'd done two years earlier.

General William Westmoreland and the military leaders who oversaw operations in Vietnam decided early on to focus on locating the enemy, destroying them, and then returning to fixed bases. It was a perfect scenario for the North Vietnamese to conduct a guerrilla war the likes of which the United States had never been engaged in. The enemy could hide in the deep jungles and mountains of South Vietnam, pick their targets, make a quick strike, and then retreat to the safety of the jungle. Without depriving them of the geography, they could do it forever. They knew that too. It was a tactical decision on the part of the United States that was doomed to failure.

"We don't have to win," Ho Chi Minh quoted prophetically. "We just have to keep punching until the enemy quits." Eventually, that's exactly what the United States did.

As the war dragged on, and we continued to fly into the same LZs again and again, questions like "What are we accomplishing here?" began to creep into my head. However, that being said, as pilots, we never let that affect our sense of duty nor our determination to get the job done. At the end of the day, our job was to support and hope-fully save the lives of our fellow Marines. Nothing, and I mean nothing, would stand in the way of that mission.

The helicopter pilots of the Vietnam War were some of the bravest and most determined men I ever met. Marine or Army, it made no difference. They often flew into horrendous situations, braving intense fire to bring in troops and supplies and take out the wounded. Around 40,000 helicopter pilots served in Vietnam—2,165 were killed and 2,712 crew members were lost. Different units faced greater risk and suffered more than others, of course. It depended on their missions and the terrain where they flew.

As bad as it could be some days, it was still the most challenging, exhilarating, and satisfying time in my life. As odd as it may sound, I still miss it, and would do it again in a heartbeat. Every time I hear a helicopter overhead, I get snapped back to my time in Vietnam. My pulse quickens, and I wish I was back inside that big old H-34 with my hand on the stick.

All Marines have a special bond. "Once a Marine, always a Marine" isn't just a slogan. It is just what it says. It's especially true of Marine helicopter pilots who flew in Vietnam. The bond between us was special indeed, and something that's flourished with time. We're a little grayer, a little heavier, and a little slower, but still have a glint in our eye or a mischievous grin peeking out from behind a mustache or beard. We still carry the confidence, the pride, and the bond that makes us Marines.

• • •

My three days were up, and it was back to work. I was refreshed and ready. Eager to get back in the air. Eager to fly with my brothers again.

I was into my eighth month, and a steady routine. We resupplied firebases on hilltop LZs in the western highlands with food, water, ammo, medicine, and everything else necessary to the outposts' operations. Those outposts were under constant sniper fire, so from time to time they'd send out patrols to clear the area of enemy units.

Those patrols invariably suffered casualties. We flew medevac missions to get those guys to field hospitals as soon as possible. Sometimes we picked them up in the LZ, but if they were in bad shape, we picked them up wherever they were. This was always more challenging due to the terrain and thick jungle canopy, not to mention it was always in outlaw country with the enemy in close proximity.

Pop a Smoke

During one such mission, we got a call from Firebase Zebra, in the western, mountainous sector. We'd just dropped off supplies at another firebase and were headed back to Phu Bai to reload for another run. A patrol from Firebase Zebra had come in contact with a VC unit, and four Marines were wounded.

I was flying as the second aircraft in a flight of two H-34s when the call came in. In the lead aircraft, Yankee Lima 15, was Major Tim Crawford and his copilot, Lieutenant Peter Graves. I was flying Yankee Lima 22 with my copilot, Jimmy Stewart. No, not the movie star, although we constantly teased him and peppered him with impressions.

As we approached Firebase Zebra, Major Crawford's radio crackled. "LZ Zebra, this is Yankee Lima 15. Over."

"Yankee Lima 15, we have four wounded in the bush about one click to our southwest and need immediate medevac." One click meant one kilometer. "The terrain is too difficult for them to get these guys back to the LZ in one piece, so we need you to pick them up where they are."

"Roger, Zebra, we're on our way," Major Crawford replied. "Please send coordinates."

The firebase sent the coordinates as we headed back toward it. Major Crawford would be the first bird in, and we'd go in after he'd gotten out safely. He was on his second tour and was an excellent pilot. He'd replaced Major Styles as operations officer when Major Styles rotated home a month earlier at the end of his tour. Crawford was a no-nonsense career officer and had the respect of the whole squadron. He led by example and wasn't afraid to do his share of the flying and risk-taking, the keys to being a good officer.

Major Crawford's voice crackled over the air. "Yankee Lima 22, each aircraft will pick up two wounded in order to keep our load light for the egress. Copy?"

"Roger that, sir," I replied. Keeping radio chatter to a minimum is important when engaged in an operation.

As we neared LZ Zebra, Major Crawford headed to the coordinates he'd received. The call sign for the ten-man team on the ground was Sentinel. They were on the same radio frequency as LZ Zebra.

As we approached the coordinates, Major Crawford keyed his mic. "Sentinel, this is Yankee Lima 15. Can you see or hear us?"

"Yankee Lima 15, this is Sentinel. We can hear you, but no visual. You're getting closer. We're down in the riverbed."

I could see the riverbed, running between two steep hillsides.

"Sentinel, we're going to fly up the riverbed," Major Crawford radioed back. "Let us know when we're overhead. Are you in contact?"

"Roger, Yankee Lima 15. We are not in contact at the moment."

The terrain was especially rugged. Finding a spot to set down and get these guys out was going to be difficult. Plus, the enemy could be anywhere down there. If they were positioned on the hillsides on either side of the riverbed, we'd be sitting ducks.

We flew up the canyon on the first pass, perhaps five hundred feet above the riverbed so the grunts could get a visual on us. We knew the VC would be able to get the same visual. We'd just made a turn, following the riverbed as it curved around the hillside to the right when the radio crackled.

"Yankee Lima 15, you're overhead," Sentinel said.

Looking down, all I could see through the treetops was the sunlit, shimmering creek snaking its way through the ravine. I keyed the mic to my crew. "Anybody see anything?"

There was a short pause. My copilot, Jimmy, responded first. "No, I don't see anything."

Next was my crew chief, Sergeant Steve Burnett. "No, sir. I can't see them either."

Shit! I thought.

Major Crawford's voice crackled over the radio. "Sentinel, can you pop smoke, please?"

"Popping smoke," came the quick reply.

We'd already been in the area long enough for the enemy to respond. We had to assume they were there, even though there had been no ground fire. They could be waiting for us to make an attempt at the medevac, when we'd be most vulnerable.

Just behind us, a trail of yellow smoke curled up from the treetops.

"Smoke behind us at six o'clock, sir," came the shout from Sergeant Burnett in the belly below me.

I turned the 34 to the right and spotted the smoke. "Yankee Lima 15, this is 22," I radioed. "We have smoke behind us."

Yankee Lima 15 turned toward the right and headed back down the riverbed. I followed. We made a wide turn, keeping the smoke in sight, looking for any possible landing spot.

Major Crawford spotted something. "Sentinel, this is Yankee Lima 15. Just below you is a turn in the creek bed with a small gravel beach, perhaps one hundred yards. Can you make it there?"

"These guys are pretty bad, but we'll make it. You'll have to give us some time."

"Sentinel, we're going to pull out of the ravine for now," Major Crawford relayed. "Call when you've reached the beach."

"Roger that, sir."

As we flew up and out of the ravine, all I could think of was how damn calm the radioman seemed under the circumstances. We weren't leaving them, but the grunts below must have felt mighty lonely as we pulled out of there.

Crawford's voice crackled again. "Yankee Lima 15, we are going to hold over the LZ until we get the word to go in. We have no air cover, so do your best to cover me when I make the approach and exit. I'll do the same during your approach. Hopefully, the bad guys are gone after the firefight with Sentinel."

"Roger, 15," I replied.

My gunner that day was Sergeant Bill "Wild Bill" Bradford, a second tour veteran with a ton of experience. I guessed his nickname came from the fact he had large eyes that were always wide open. With his shaved head and a scar that covered the whole of his left cheek, he indeed looked like a wild man. Or perhaps it had something to do with his personality, which matched his look. In any event, I was glad to have his experience along today.

I keyed my mic. "Sergeant, did you hear that last communication from Major Crawford?"

"Yessir, I did. I'm ready."

"Good. If he gets any ground fire, everyone keep your eyes peeled for its source, and let me know. I'll get us into position to give suppressive fire."

Three "Rogers" followed from the crew.

The H-34 had limited effectiveness for that type of action, with only the one M60 machine gun on its right side. But it's what we had, and we'd sure as hell make the best of it.

Thirty minutes later, Sentinel called. It had been difficult to carry the wounded Marines down the rocky creek bed to the turn in the river, but they'd made it. There was still no enemy contact. I had my fingers and toes crossed.

"Yankee Lima 15, this is Sentinel. We're in position."

"Sentinel, this is Yankee Lima 15," Major Crawford replied. "We are inbound. Have the two most severely wounded ready to load first. I'm

124

gonna land in the creek bed. Have your wounded staged at the tree line around the gravel beach on the right side of the creek. Yankee Lima 22 will come in for the other two wounded once I'm clear of the LZ. Put up a perimeter for fire support in case we need it. Copy?"

"Roger, sir."

"Yankee Lima 22," Major Crawford said. "You ready?"

"Yessir, we are," I answered. "I'll follow you down and cover."

"Here we go," he replied.

I could see the gunner in his 34 clear the M60. I ordered Wild Bill to do the same. A short burst from ours followed.

Major Crawford began his descent into the ravine, heading up the creek bed. I could see the small gravel beach at the turn in the river. We stayed a safe distance behind and above in order to respond to ground fire.

The only realistic approach was a simple glide slope into the LZ. The close hillsides didn't allow for many evasive maneuvers. It was a vulnerable approach, but there was no choice.

Five hundred feet, three hundred feet, two hundred feet. Major Crawford approached the creek bed and was down. I could see Marines carrying two stretchers to the bird.

The next moment, gunfire erupted from the hillside to the left of the creek bed. I could see the rounds chewing up the water and the ground around Yankee Lima 15. The grunts immediately returned fire with all they had. We could clearly see the fire was coming from one hundred yards or so up the hillside.

I immediately gained some altitude, flying over and past Yankee Lima 15, and made a hard left-hand turn to get us in position to return fire. I didn't have to tell Wild Bill anything. As soon as he had an angle, he opened up with the M60, maintaining a constant barrage as I made a quick pass. I felt a few rounds come our way, but the enemy was more focused on the H-34 on the ground. It was an easier target, and they'd clog the LZ if they killed the pilots or incapacitated the aircraft. In effect, the wounded wouldn't be able to get out.

The grunts on the ground were pouring it on as Major Crawford's voice came over the radio. "Yankee Lima 15 is departing the LZ."

As I passed over, I turned the bird again to the left, heading back down the ravine for one more suppressive fire run and then back up the ravine toward the LZ. I saw Major Crawford gaining altitude. He made a left turn and began his gun run on the hillside.

I fully focused on the small LZ and getting us in there. The gunfire seemed to have lessened as we reached about fifty yards out. I threaded our way up the ravine, through the trees, and over the creek bed. As we reached the gravel bar, I flared the nose up, pulled in some collective and power, and established a four-foot hover. I set the aircraft down in the creek as a few scattered rounds hit the water and ground in front of us. Four Marines scrambled out of the tree line, carrying the two wounded Marines on makeshift stretchers made of ponchos. They climbed inside within seconds. Just then, a new fusillade of bullets slammed into the 34.

I looked over at my copilot, Jimmy. He gave me the thumbs-up. I keyed the mic to my crew chief. "Steve, are you and Bill okay?"

"Yeah, but one of the wounded took a round in the leg. I gotta go."

I reached down to lift the collective and get us out of the zone. My right foot slipped along the floor. It was covered in blood. *Shit! Am I hit?* I thought. I didn't feel like it.

Just then, a stream of blood shot up through the opening between the pilot seats from the belly below. I looked down and saw Steve Burnett trying to put a tourniquet on the leg of the Marine who'd been hit. I couldn't hear it, but I could see the scream escape his face.

"Yankee Lima 22 is leaving the zone," I called out.

I lifted us into a hover and got us airborne and headed up the ravine. From what I could tell, the gunfire had stopped. I made a right turn and sped back down the ravine to gain speed and altitude. A few minutes later, we were at three thousand feet and headed back to the 22nd Surgical Field Hospital at Phu Bai.

I keyed the mic to my crew chief. "How are we doing down there, Sergeant?"

"Sir," Bill answered, "Steve is still working on the tourniquet. We've got a lot of blood back here. Both men are in serious condition. Pedal to the metal, sir."

We were ten minutes out. I radioed Major Crawford. "Yankee Lima 22, this is 15. I've got two critical." I knew the major would radio ahead to the field hospital at Phu Bai to give them our situation. Seconds later, I heard his call.

"Phu Bai Med, this is Yankee Lima 15. We're inbound with two aircraft and four wounded. Three critical, and one stable. We're five minutes out."

"Yankee Lima 15, this is Phu Bai Med. We copy."

12. *The Twilight Zone*

The 22nd Surgical Field Hospital at Phu Bai was run by the Army, on the western side of the runway. The landing pad there was big enough for several helicopters, so we made our approach in formation and landed together. Four teams of stretcher bearers came running from the main building to unload the wounded and get them inside. It was over in minutes.

Major Crawford's voice crackled. "Yankee Lima 22, let's get back to the flight line and regroup."

"Roger that, sir."

We picked our birds up into a hover at the same time and made a formation departure to the right, heading just across the runway toward our flight line. We landed and taxied into the parking revetment.

Jimmy and I shut down the aircraft and climbed out. We counted twelve holes in the fuselage, but none in the engine compartment, which meant we were good to go when necessary.

I looked at Steve and Wild Bill. "You guys okay?" It had been a tough mission, especially with the two critically wounded Marines. Trying to keep them alive until we got them to the hospital had been tough physically and emotionally for my crew. They'd never admit it, however.

"Yeah, we're good, LT," was all Steve said.

Neither of them was in the mood for much else. They turned and began filling buckets of water to wash away the blood that covered the floor of the bird.

"Well, good job, men." I left them with their thoughts.

Major Crawford and I made our way to the operations shack to fill out our after-action reports. As we walked, he looked over at me. "Good flying today, Rick."

"You too, sir. I'd be glad to be your wingman any day."

He smiled, and we entered the operations shack. Thirty minutes earlier, we'd been in a shit sandwich. Now we hunched over a table, filling out paperwork in a whole different universe. It was always difficult to wrap my head around the drastic transition between a mission like that and being back at the base in a safe and secure environment within a matter of minutes. It was like an episode of *The Twilight Zone*. Reality and imagination were difficult to separate. In fact, my whole tour in Vietnam seemed like a full season of Rod Serling's show.

13

Final Days

By July 1969, military leaders decided HMM-362 would be drawn down and cease combat operations in Vietnam. The determination came in large part to the age and inefficiency of the H-34. Some pilots were transferred and retrained on the H-46, or in some cases the HU-1, the "Huey." It felt strange to watch our pilots leave the squadron for new assignments. Guys we'd lived with and flown with for months were gone. But those of us still with HMM-362 still managed to keep in touch with them.

One day, my good friend Pete Peterson walked in and sat down at the table where four of us were playing a lackluster game of poker. It was a day like any day, hot and humid, with no flight operations scheduled. We sat around writing letters, shooting the breeze, or playing poker.

"I just heard that Ted Bennington was shot down yesterday," Pete said. Ted had been transferred to HMM-265 a month earlier. "He was on a medevac and crashed trying to get into the LZ. Apparently the 46 burst into flames on impact. No one made it out."

We all stared at the table.

"Goddamn it!" I yelled.

Those of us still flying the H-34 knew our flying days were coming to an end soon, and our chances of going home were vastly improving. However, watching our friends transfer to other squadrons and continue to be at great risk was a bitter pill to swallow. In some ways, I felt guilty that I wasn't sharing that risk. Like we all did, I wanted to give my full measure of effort. We began feeling as though we'd been benched while the rest of the team continued to play. I hated it. It was, of course, just a matter of operational staffing decisions, but that proved little comfort. Many of us asked to be transferred to any available squadron. But the staffing decisions were out of our control. We were destined to be the last pilots flying for HMM-362.

13. Final Days

Two weeks later, a pilot named Woody Tillerson burst into the hooch with an incredible story. His voice rose with excitement as he began talking. "Hey, guys, you're not going to believe this! Roger got shot down during a resupply mission near the Laotian boarder." Roger Steele had also been transferred to HMM-262 to fly the 46. "I guess the NVA who took them down made their way to the wreckage to check on survivors and salvage whatever they could. Roger was still strapped in the aircraft, covered in blood with a severe head wound. The NVA stripped him of his maps, weapons, and everything else they could find in the aircraft. The rest of the crew didn't make it, and the NVA left him for dead as well. But that son of a bitch was still alive. Maybe they thought he was dead because of all the blood. He apparently regained consciousness, got his ass out of the wreckage, and crawled out of the ravine and over the ridge. He got picked up by a patrol from the LZ he was trying to get to. Can you fucking believe that?"

"Are you sure about that, Woody?" Pete asked.

"Yeah, I saw him in the field hospital. That's one tough son of a bitch, that's for sure. They're going to ship him home. He had a terrible head wound, but, hey, he's going home."

Good for you, Roger, you lucky bastard, was all I could think.

We all headed over to the O Club to celebrate Roger's good luck.

• • •

August 6, 1969, was the date of the last combat mission for HMM-362. It was a sad day for all of us. We wanted to keep flying. To be in the action. To do our part. HMM-362 was the first Marine helicopter squadron in Vietnam, back in 1962. Seven years later, it was over for the "Ugly Angels." A part of Marine Corps history was fading into the books. Our squadron flew thousands of missions during the war and lost 33 pilots and crew members.

On that last day, we all gathered in the operations shack. The squadron had been reduced to about half its size by then. There were only eight aircraft going out that day. The CO, Colonel Matthews, assembled the entire squadron—pilots, crew chiefs, gunners, admin personnel, and support staff. Everybody was there.

At 0800, the entire squadron stood in formation on the flight line. All our H-34s were parked in a row behind Colonel Matthews, who was standing in the back of a jeep. U.S. and Marine Corps flags ruffled in the light breeze behind him.

Pop a Smoke

His voice boomed over the crowd. "Gentlemen, this is an historic day for our squadron. As the first Marine helicopter squadron to serve in Vietnam, HMM-362 will always be a part of Marine Corps history. Never forget what this squadron has accomplished over the past seven years, and the honor we share by being part of that. We are now, and always will be, the 'Ugly Angels.' Keep in your hearts the memory of those we lost, those who gave the ultimate sacrifice for their squadron and country. Today, we fly together for the last time. It's an honor to have served with you. Fly safe."

A thunderous "OOOORRRRAAHHHH" boomed across the tarmac. As bittersweet as it was, it was a proud moment for all of us.

The day was even more special for me because I was flying with my good friend Pete Peterson. Another good friend of ours, Ron Janousek, had been transferred a week earlier to HML 367, a Huey squadron based at Phu Bai. It was odd not having him with us on that last day.

The CO had arranged for the eight aircraft to make a formation rolling takeoff. We climbed inside and cranked up our 34s.

The CO's voice came over the airwaves. "Tower, this is Yankee Lima 11. Permission to take the runway for an eight-aircraft formation departure."

"Yankee Lima 11, this is Phu Bai tower. Permission granted, and it's an honor to be here for this. Godspeed. Semper Fi."

"Roger, tower. Semper Fi."

We taxied out two by two, following the CO and XO in Yankee Lima 12. Once in formation of four lines of two aircraft each, Colonel Matthews's voice came over the radio. "HMM-362 rolling."

Pete and I were in the third row. We could see the first two 34s taxiing down the runway, increasing in speed. The second row followed just behind. I kept my eye on them as we began taxiing forward as well. By then, the two lead aircraft had gained enough speed that their noses had pitched forward, and their tail wheels were off the ground. In another second, the next two aircraft moved faster down the runway and lifted off simultaneously. Each row followed in sequence. I'd taken more than a few rolling takeoffs, but never with eight aircraft at once. It was amazing. I wish I'd thought to have someone film it.

Once airborne, each flight of two headed for its mission. Our objectives were relatively easy—some resupply drops, some admin runs, and some routine medevacs, meaning no hot zones. Pete and I switched off flying to ensure we split the time and chores equally.

13. *Final Days*

At the end of the day, as we approached Phu Bai, I keyed the mic. "Hey, pal, how about we both have our hands on the control for the approach and landing?"

"That would be nice." Pete's voice showed his emotions were running high too.

With that came my last landing in the grand old H-34, with my pilot friend and my aircraft friend. We landed, taxied to the parking revetment, and slowly shut her down.

Climbing out, I gave the side of good old Yankee Lima 13 a couple of pats. "Thanks, old gal," I whispered. "I'm gonna miss you."

Pete and I walked around the aircraft one last time and then stood in front of our crewmen. They were my favorite crewmen, Stacy Brinkman and Keg Johnson. Pete and I gave them the best salutes we had.

"Gentlemen, it has been an incredible honor to fly and serve with you. I hope when we all get home, we'll have a chance to get together to drink some beers and swap some lies."

They came to attention, something their breed of airman didn't often do. Stacy returned the salute with a smile on his face. "The honor is ours, LT. But if we do have that chance, bring your wallet. You know how Keg got his nickname, right?"

"I'll remember that. Take care, guys. Semper Fi."

Pete and I turned and headed for the operations shack for our last after-action paperwork.

Three days later, on August 9, Pete and I were sitting in the hooch playing gin. The rest of the pilots from our hooch were out and about, including our best pal, Ron Janousek, who'd been transferred to the Huey squadron.

There was a knock on the screen door, and a voice rang out. "Staff Sergeant Tanner here. Permission to enter, sirs."

"Yeah, come on in, Sergeant," Pete said.

Sergeant Tanner entered and stood in front of the table. He gave us a salute, which we returned. He looked slightly rigid. "Gentlemen, the CO would like to see you in his office."

I looked at Pete with raised eyebrows. "What did you do now?" I joked.

"Well, let me think. Nope, nothing I can remember." He scoffed. "It was probably something you did."

"Tell the CO we're on our way, Sergeant," I said.

"Yessir," Sergeant Tanner replied. He saluted again, turned, and exited the hooch.

Pete and I looked at one another again, shrugged, and tossed the cards on the table. We straightened ourselves up a bit and headed down the plank walkway to squadron headquarters. It was midday and the heat was brutal, as usual. By the time we reached headquarters, we were bathed in sweat. So much for sprucing up.

We entered, and Sergeant Tanner stood with another salute. "The CO is expecting you. Go right in."

I felt a knot in my stomach. Something wasn't right.

Pete and I entered the office and stood in front of the CO's desk. We saluted, and he returned the gesture and nodded at the two chairs in front of his desk. "Have a seat, gentlemen."

The office was small and simple. The overhead fan creaked with each slow revolution, barely disturbing the hot air. There wasn't enough of a breeze to even disrupt the flies that buzzed overhead. On the wall behind the desk was a picture of President Johnson. An American flag stood on a pole in a stand next to it. Toward the right was a picture taken earlier in the year of the squadron pilots in front of an H-34. Toward the left were a number of framed pictures of H-34s in the field. Along the left wall was a map table.

"Gentlemen, I'm sorry to tell you that Lieutenant Janousek was lost in action today." He paused, looking at us, then shared the details of what had happened.

I felt as though I'd been transported out of my body. I could hear his voice, but his words didn't register. It sounded as though he was at the other end of a long hallway. Neither Pete nor I said anything. The CO continued for a while longer, and I returned to earth as he concluded.

"I know the three of you were good friends, and I'm sorry to have to give you this news. If you need anything, let me know." He stood and stretched out his hand.

Pete and I stood, shook his hand, and saluted. Pete managed to say, "Thank you, sir," as we turned and walked from the office.

We passed through the outer screen door into the blinding sun and blistering heat, then walked back to the hooch in silence. Pete and I entered and gave one another a hug. There was nothing to say.

I looked at Ron's cubicle just behind us. We'd said, "Fly safe today, brother," that morning as he left for his mission. There was a hole the size of a bowling ball inside my chest.

13. Final Days

It was several days before Pete and I were able to read the report of the incident and the details surrounding Ron's death.

Ron had been transferred to HML 367 one week earlier. On August 6, he was flying as copilot in a Huey with Major Tom Hill on an emergency recon extraction mission inside the Laotian border. There were two Huey "slicks," or troop carriers, four Cobra gunships, and two Vietnamese "Kingbee" H-34s on the mission. A platoon-size Marine recon unit was in heavy contact and required immediate help.

The incident report read as follows:

> Once on-site, the lead Cobra was in contact with the recon team, which was in a fierce firefight with a large NVA unit on the ground. The team was next to a river at the bottom of a ravine. The lead Cobra, piloted by Captain Michael J. Brokovich, made a pass over the ridgeline above the river, trying to locate the recon team, and received heavy ground fire. Pulling up and away from the ridgeline, he radioed to Major Hill to inform him where the fire had come from and where the enemy was concentrated.
>
> To Captain Brokovich's astonishment, Major Hill flew over the same ridgeline and was hit by heavy ground fire. The Huey was hit in the engine and immediately caught fire. He radioed a Mayday, that he was hit and losing power. He moved the stricken aircraft toward the river in an attempt to land in the water and put out the fire.
>
> The team on the ground directed Major Hill to a clearing downriver if he could make it. As they approached the clearing, Ron's voice screamed over the radio, "I'm on fire! I'm on fire!" Those were his last words.
>
> At seventy-five feet over the river, the tail boom broke off and the Huey inverted and crashed into the fast-moving river.
>
> Major Hill and the crew chief, Corporal J.J. Dean, were able to exit the aircraft, were swept downstream about one hundred meters, and got to shore on the opposite side of the river from the enemy.
>
> While the four Cobras laid down suppressive fire, the lead South Vietnamese H-34 Kingbee, piloted by Dai Uy Ahn, located, and rescued both Major Hill and Corporal Dean under intense ground fire. The door gunner, who had also been able to exit the aircraft, was seen onshore alive and well. According to the pilot in one of the Cobras overhead, Corporal Dean, who was known as a strong swimmer, went back into the river to the wreckage in an attempt to rescue Lieutenant Janousek. (Lieutenant Janousek) was not seen again.
>
> After rescuing both Major Hill and Corporal Dean, Dai Uy Ahn flew his H-34 back to the wreckage in an attempt to find the two missing crewmen as the four Cobras continued to lay down suppressive fire. In an incredible feat of airmanship, Dai Uy Ahn, while hovering over the wreckage, engaged his front wheel through the window of the Huey and picked it up to see if his crew chief could see inside. There was no one inside. He placed the

wreckage back in the river and disengaged from the Huey. The entire time, the Kingbee was under continuous enemy fire.

The mission leader turned his attention to the embattled recon team, still fighting for survival. All aircraft returned to Quang Tri to rearm and refuel. Afterward, they successfully extracted the reconnaissance team without incident. Afterward, and again the next morning, Captain Frank Cuddy led a search and rescue (SAR) flight of gunships to the site to continue the search for Corporal Kane and First Lieutenant Janousek. All attempts were driven away by intense small arms and automatic weapons fire from the enemy. The aircrews observed a large number of communist troops along the riverbanks, in the clearings, and trees. They also saw ten to twenty small boats in the river near the wreckage and enemy forces obviously searching it. Because the region was under total enemy control, any ground search by US personnel was impossible.

When the search was terminated, Ron and Bruce Kane were listed as Missing in Action. After thirty-three days, the squadron commander reviewed all known information and changed both men's status to Killed in Action/Body Not Recovered (and probably not recoverable).

Pete and I spent part of the next day gathering Ron's personal effects to send home to his wife and two small daughters. We wrote them a note and placed it with his belongings. I don't even remember what I wrote. We'd lost friends before but losing "Hauser" was especially difficult. It remains difficult even today. August 6 was Pete's and my final day flying combat. August 9 was Ron's final day, period. Rest in peace, my brother.

14

Departure

I left the communications building and trudged through the mud under sheets of driving rain. August had brought record heat, and a monsoon that had rendered the base at Phu Bai a soggy, stinking quagmire—one that threatened to claim my boots with each step I took.

Across the compound I trudged. I was so relieved to reach squadron headquarters that I didn't even care about the trail of brown I brought inside with me. I shrugged at the duty sergeant, who rolled his eyes as he escorted me into the CO's office.

I gave Colonel Matthews the customary salute, which he returned.

"Here's the report you requested, sir," I said, handing it over. "I have to tell you, the files were in such bad shape, I'm not sure how much help they'll be."

With the squadron no longer engaged in flight operations, the remaining officers had been assigned tasks, however meaningless, to keep us from going stir crazy. Mine was to organize and translate the daily classified communications between the squadron and a variety of other commands. For two weeks running, I'd been wading through piles of barely decipherable paperwork, unable to make much sense of what had been left unattended for months. I was relieved to be finished, even if my report was basically useless.

"Don't worry about it, Lieutenant. I knew it'd be impossible to straighten out." A wry smile appeared on the colonel's face. "But, hey, it gave you something to do for a while, right?"

Annoyed but trying not to show it, I gave a slight nod.

"I got something else for you, though." His smile disappeared, giving way to an expression that told me that *something else* wasn't anything good.

Every man who ever served in Vietnam dreamed of the day he'd get to go home. After eight or nine months, sometimes longer, we'd begin short-timer calendars, marking off the days to our hoped-for departure. We all had a vision of the day we'd board that big commercial airliner that would take us the hell out of Vietnam and ferry us back home. The big silver bird. It was a vision that gave us hope. A picture we held in our minds. A light at the end of the tunnel.

"Lieutenant, I need you to escort two companies of Marines to Okinawa. You'll be traveling by ship. You'll depart in three days. Get your gear together and report to Da Nang. That's where you'll disembark." He stood up and handed me some paperwork. "Here are your orders. You'll report to the commanding officer at Okinawa upon your arrival. Any questions?"

I was stunned by the sudden change in plans. *No silver bird? A ship? What?* There wasn't much I could say. *This was how my tour would end?* I was sure the colonel could read the confusion on my face. I wasn't sure how to feel. As ready as I was to go home, I still wanted to fly. I'd hoped to be reassigned to another squadron to finish my tour, like some of our other pilots. That obviously wasn't going to happen. It was over. No more flying. I felt my heart drop to the bottom of my stomach. Everything had changed in a millisecond.

"Lieutenant, you had a good tour and performed more than admirably. You served with honor and distinction. Your country and the Marine Corps are in your debt. Keep that in mind." He paused slightly. "Dismissed."

I stood, still locked in disbelief. I gathered myself. "Colonel, is there any chance I could get reassigned to another squadron, sir? I still have two months left on my tour, and I really want to finish it out flying."

"Sorry, Lieutenant. I know how you feel, but those are your orders."

All I could do was step back, offer a, "Yessir," and give the CO a salute, which he returned. I thought for a moment and with some controlled emotion mustered, "It has been an honor, sir." I turned on my heel and exited the office.

Walking back to my hooch in the rain, I felt dejected and somehow rejected. The finality of it all weighed heavily on me. *In the end*, I thought, *I'm going home.* Besides, escorting two companies of Marines to Okinawa on a ship might be kind of interesting. Not everyone gets that kind of assignment. And I'd still fly home at some point. *Okay, so let's make the best of it.*

I spent the next two days gathering my few possessions and spending time with Pete. We mostly played cards, talked about the good times, and some of the not so good, and of course, put in significant time at the O Club.

Then it was August 27. It had finally stopped raining. Steam rose from the metal roofs of the hooches as the sun turned them once again into frying pans. I said my goodbyes to Pete and the other two pilots still in the hooch. We assured one another we'd stay in touch and get together often.

Then there was Han. She was standing at the door, dressed in her usual black pajamas with a big straw hat shielding her face in shadow. She'd been a huge part of our lives. She loved us, and we loved her. She'd washed our filthy clothes, cleaned our dirty hut, and sewed, cooked, and cared for us as though we were her family. And we were. She'd joked with us, always telling us, "You numba one," if we pleased her in some way, or "You numba ten," if we transgressed in some fashion. What would happen to her when we were gone? I worried for her.

As I reached the screen door where she stood, I dropped my duffel bag and sat on it so I was eye level with her. Tears ran down her cheeks.

I took her birdlike hands in mine, and with moist eyes of my own, I said something I'd been practicing for three days. *"Tôi sẽ luôn nhớ bạn Cảm ơn bạn đã là mẹ của tôi trong năm nay."* It meant: "I will always miss you. Thank you for being my mother this year."

I gave her a little box wrapped in brown paper, tied with a red ribbon. Inside was a multicolored scarf I'd purchased in Da Nang, the St. Christopher's medal my Aunt Pat gave me before I left for Vietnam, and about one hundred U.S. dollars in Vietnamese currency. As she stared down at the box, I gave her a long hug. Then I stood up and walked through the door with my duffel bag. The long, low moan that came as I left was the only time I ever heard her cry.

Walking down the mud-caked path between the rows of dirt-covered hooches and bunkers for the last time was surprisingly bittersweet. A stiff breeze swirled the hateful brown sand into a cloud of fine dust. It seemed Phu Bai was giving me one last sarcastic goodbye. As ugly and primitive as my surroundings were, this place still had been, well, home. I'd heard a lot of laughter in those ramshackle huts, and I knew I'd probably never experience that level of camaraderie again.

As I headed for the jeep waiting for me at the end of the path, I thought of the friends who'd been sent in all directions as the squadron counted down its final days. I thought of all my friends who wouldn't

(From left) Hauser, me and Pete, with Han (author's collection).

be going home at all. Especially Hauser. The gang was gone. I was once again on my own. Stronger, wiser, and certainly humbler. I threw my bag into the jeep and nodded at the corporal behind the wheel.

We drove out to the flight line, where an H-46 was waiting to fly down to Da Nang. I gave a quick salute to the pilot, which he returned as I boarded. I wondered how long he'd been in-country and what his future held. Oddly enough, I'd never been in the belly of a 46 before, and the relatively short flight to Da Nang gave me a taste of what the grunts experienced on every mission. As a pilot, I had a great view of every-thing around me. Inside the belly of the 46 felt like being in a window-less cargo van. The deafening noise of the two jet engines overhead and the vibration of the twin-rotor fuselage was horrendous. I could imagine what the grunts thought as they headed to who knows where and who knows what crammed inside that hellish tin can.

We landed at Da Nang, and a small bus picked us up on the tarmac. The six of us rode to the headquarters building, to be briefed on the next step of our journeys. One at a time, we were ushered into an office, and a major walked us through our orders.

When my turn came, I walked inside, saluted, and stood at attention.

"At ease, Lieutenant." The major continued to stare at the papers on his desk. "Looks like you're going for a boat ride. Probably not how you expected to leave this garden spot, huh?" He finally looked up, and I noticed the scar on his face and the Purple Heart tucked in the three rows of ribbons on his chest.

"No, sir, not exactly."

"Well, at least you're going home, right?"

"Yessir."

He shifted into rapid speech, suddenly all business. "All right, here's the deal. Tomorrow at 0800, you will report to the dock at the harbor, Pier Four. Report to the duty officer on the USS *Lyon County*. It's a big-ass LST. You know what an LST is, Lieutenant?"

"Well, kinda, yessir," I mumbled. Shit, I knew what they were, and I knew for sure this trip wasn't going to be a pleasure cruise.

"Okay, this baby is going to be loaded to the gills with all manner of cargo. Two companies of Marines will be billeted in the shitty quarters below decks. Your job is to look after them and try not to lose any on the way to Okinawa. Understood?"

"Yessir."

"Once you get to Okinawa, report to Marine Corps headquarters for further orders. Any questions?"

"No, sir."

I had more than a few, but I knew better than to ask. I'd have to wait and see what I could get from the Squids (a not-so-friendly term for the boys in the Navy) after I boarded.

The major passed my orders across his desk, then looked down at the next pile of papers. "Goodbye. *Bon voyage*," he said without looking up.

Yeah, bon voyage to you too, sir, I thought. I saluted to the top of his head, then made a quick heel turn and found the door.

He was probably a nice enough guy. He'd obviously done at least two tours, had seen it all for sure, and was undoubtedly unhappy being tied to a desk. Yeah, well, I wasn't getting my wish to keep flying, so what the hell. As I exited the headquarters building, I was reminded of our old saying: "United States Marine Corps: one good deal after another. OORRAAHH!"

I hefted my bag and asked the duty driver outside to take me to the Bachelor Officers' Quarters. During the drive over, I couldn't help but notice that even in Da Nang, the unmistakable stench of burning shitters permeated the air. I remembered how I'd noticed it almost a year earlier when I'd deplaned. It would probably be the last thing I'd notice as I shipped out. At least I was away from the dust, mud, and filth of Phu Bai.

I was elated to spend the night in the BOQ—it meant a real bed with a mattress, and real showers as hot and long as I wanted, plus real food just like in a restaurant. I checked in and treated myself to the longest and most luxuriously hot shower I'd taken in almost a year. It was glorious. I shaved, donned my least-wrinkled set of utilities, and headed to eat at the officers' mess. No writing my name in dust on a plate. White tablecloth. Even a waiter, for God's sake!

I chose to eat alone that night. I didn't want to share the moment, for some reason. I ordered a martini, a rare T-bone steak, a baked potato with all the trimmings, and, if you can believe it, actual fresh, or close enough, green beans. Every sip and every bite was glorious.

After a big slice of cheesecake and another martini, I left a heavy tip and headed to the bar. I'm not sure what time I collapsed into my bed, but I remember it was like falling into a cloud.

I must have had brains enough to ask the desk clerk to wake me at 0600 and insist he knock loudly because the door almost came off its hinges as I struggled to bark out, "Okay, okay, okay!" through the fog of a serious hangover.

My mouth tasted like I'd swallowed a dead animal. Somewhere in my head was a helicopter at full throttle. Lots of toothpaste, a long, cold shower, three aspirin, and a fresh change of clothes thanks to the overnight laundry facilities, and I was ready for breakfast. I may have been hung over, but I wasn't going to miss the opportunity for one more pass at the officers' mess menu. Good food was a luxury, and I knew the LST fare would be less than memorable.

15

Boat Ride from Hell

The duty driver dropped me off at 0730 at Pier Four. Knowing I was leaving Vietnam, he delivered a salute. "Good luck, and a safe trip home, sir. Semper Fi."

"Thanks." I returned his salute. "Good luck to you too. Semper Fi."

There was no mistaking the USS *Lyon County*. She took up most of the pier. At 382 feet long and 50 feet wide, her gray hulk loomed three stories above the dock. The LST was developed in World War II as a cargo vessel that could pack fifty tanks into its bay, then cross the Atlantic Ocean and deliver them onto the beaches of North Africa. Her bow wasn't pointed like all the other ships in the Navy, but rather a flat cargo ramp to allow for loading and unloading vehicles. As a result, her top speed was about eleven knots in normal seas. Hell, I used to row a single rowing shell six knots in normal conditions. Then there was the fact that the LST's flat bottom meant its stability on an open sea was less than optimum, to put it mildly. I'd soon learn just how unstable it could be.

I walked up the gangway to the main deck, and, as customary, saluted the flag and then the duty officer waiting at the top of the ramp.

"Welcome aboard, Lieutenant," he said, returning my salute. He motioned to a sailor standing next to him. "Seaman Reynolds here will escort you to your quarters. Your Marines are due to arrive and board in thirty minutes. The captain is on the bridge when you're ready."

"Thank you, Ensign."

I nodded at Seaman Reynolds, and we headed to the superstructure at the stern of the LST. Up a couple of exterior metal stairways, through a metal hatch (doorway), down a short galley way (hall), and Seaman Reynolds opened the door to my quarters.

The room was almost comically tight, which was typical of Navy vessels. There was an upper and lower bunk on the far wall, while the other held a small built-in table and bench seats able to accommodate two men. At the other side of the space was a small head (bathroom), with a toilet, shower, and sink.

I'd spent two months of my tour cooped up on the *Iwo Jima*, as HMM-362 had directed flight operations from that old World War II aircraft carrier. I'd hated it then, and I sure wasn't going to like this much more. Thank God I hadn't joined the Navy. The only good news was the major who'd given me my orders had said it would only take three to four days to reach Okinawa.

"Let's go see the captain," I said as I threw my bag on the lower bunk.

I followed Seaman Reynolds up another flight of metal stairs and entered the bridge. The captain stood with his back to me, dressed in his freshly starched white uniform, looking over the length of the ship toward shore. I had a momentary flashback to the day I'd stood in front of the Navy recruiting officer. I remembered how much I'd admired those sharp dress whites. *Christ*, I thought, *that seems like more than a lifetime ago.*

I came to attention, rendered a salute, and held it. "Lieutenant Gehweiler reporting, sir."

He turned around slowly and looked me over, then returned my salute. "Welcome aboard, Lieutenant. You ever been aboard a Navy vessel before?"

He wore the rank of commander, and was probably in his late fifties, and six feet tall, with a squared jaw, and salt-and-pepper hair barely visible under his gold-braided officer's hat. His chest bore three rows of ribbons, which I had no way of identifying since they were Navy honors. His nametag read *Denton*.

"Yes, sir, my helicopter squadron operated for two months on the *Iwo Jima* off Da Nang."

"I see." He continued to stare into my eyes. "Well, you may find that the open ocean is a different animal than the waters offshore of Da Nang." He turned and looked back over the length of the ship. "Your two companies of Marines will come aboard shortly. Their quarters are very cramped. You may want to review them before they board. Seaman Reynolds will show you the way. Let me know if there's anything you require for their welfare during the voyage."

"Yessir. Thank you, sir."

Seaman Reynolds gave me a slight nod to the left and we exited the bridge. We descended stairway after stairway down into the bowels of the ship. Finally, he opened a hatchway that led into the main cargo hold.

The cavernous space was three stories tall and full of military trucks and vehicles of every description. They were fully loaded with gear and packed so tightly together you couldn't have stuck a toothpick between them. We inched sideways through the narrow opening between the vehicles and the bulkhead (wall) until we reached another door facing aft as we neared the bow of the ship. Reynolds opened the door and motioned for me to go through.

In front of me was a room, more like a chamber, perhaps six feet wide and maybe 150 feet long. On each wall was a three-tier set of canvas bunks on metal frames with no mattresses. A three-foot-wide aisle separated the rows of racks and led to four toilet stalls at the end of the room. Bare light bulbs with metal cages hung from the low ceiling every thirty feet or so. The metal room reverberated with the sound of workers making final preparations. I shuddered to think what it would sound like once we were underway, and the engines began their cacophony. It seemed like a freaking torture chamber already.

I turned and stared at Reynolds, my mouth open and eyebrows raised as high as possible. He shrugged and shook his head slowly as if to say, "Yeah, I know. It sucks. But it is what it is."

"Jesus!" I barked. "You gotta be kidding me. It's like a tomb. I hope to God they can last four days in here."

"Well, sir, they will get break time on deck in small groups, and there will be breaks to go to the mess for meals."

"Get me back up topside. I need to be there when my Marines show up."

I was steamed. Those Marines had been in-country for who knows how long. They'd endured every conceivable hardship imaginable. And *this* was how they got to leave? Crammed like sardines inside a can, without sunlight, pounded by unrelenting banging and crashing? Oh yeah, I forgot: "United States Marine Corps: one good deal after another."

I was determined to do whatever I could to make the best of it for them. I had my own little room. I'd be fine. They, on the other hand, would have one more ordeal to endure.

Reynolds and I headed to the top of the ship. I thought about what he'd said about break time for the Marines topside. Hell, there was no topside. It was wall-to-wall, double-stacked, huge metal Conex boxes.

The only space was a three-foot area between the huge metal containers and the outer railing. There was enough room to maybe have a cigarette and stretch your legs for a minute. I prayed the next four days would pass quickly.

As I stood with the duty officer at the top of the gangway, I looked down the dock and could see a line of trucks headed our way. As they pulled up, two gunnery sergeants hopped out of the first two trucks, barking orders. In short order, two companies of Marines in field packs and weapons stood in formation. The first gunnery sergeant jogged up the gangway and popped a salute to the flag and then another to the duty officer and me.

He was about five foot ten and maybe 160 pounds. Not an ounce of fat. His tanned and weather-beaten skin was stretched tight over his angular face. His uniform looked as though it had been spray-starched on him. Not a crease out of place, even in that heat. A quick glance at his three rows of ribbons revealed two Bronze Stars and three Purple Hearts. This was who you wanted in charge. "Gunnery Sergeant Thomas reporting, sir," he barked.

"Welcome aboard, Gunny. Before we board the men, I need you to take a look at their quarters." I wasn't looking forward to this.

"No need, sir. I know what they are. Not my first time aboard an LST."

"Yeah, I imagine not, Gunny." I realized he already knew what was at hand and didn't even blink. "You need anything from me, you ask. Okay?"

Hell, he didn't need anything from me other than to stay out of his way. In the Marine Corps, gunnery sergeants were gods. Even generals gave them deference. Gunnery sergeants had put in the time and shouldered the load in war and peace since the beginning. They were the fire within the engine.

"Thanks, Lieutenant." His voice was raspy. "We'll be fine."

"Very well. Carry on." There wasn't much else to say.

After another exchange of salutes, he returned down the gangway.

In a few moments, two companies of Marines headed up the gangway and then into the bowels of the ship. As I watched them disappear, I imagined they were being devoured by a giant iron beast. My hangover was returning. I needed a drink. But there was no booze allowed on Navy ships. How long was it to Okinawa?

We weighed anchor an hour later and left Da Nang Harbor. The first day was uneventful. Though my room was small, it was comfortable. Gunnery Sergeant Thomas and the other gunnery sergeant, whose name was Tyler, were quartered across the hall in an identical room. Gunnery Sergeant Tyler was about five foot ten and built like a brick shithouse. He was as weather-beaten as Thomas but with a voice that sounded like a bullhorn. He reminded me of the drill sergeants at Quantico. Sergeant Tyler's uniform was as crisp and perfect as his partner's, and displayed three rows of ribbons, including two Purple Hearts. I thought of the men as TNT—I was sure when the shit had hit the fan in the bush, they'd been at the heart of the action.

Two hours after we departed, I saw Gunny Thomas emerge from below decks.

"How are the men doin', Gunny?"

"Men are fine, sir. Bit cramped, but everything is squared away."

"Gunny, I know you probably want this skinny-ass aviator lieutenant to stay the hell out of your way, but I'm here to give you any help you may need. Just saying."

"Yes, sir. I appreciate it. I'll let you know if I do, but my Marines will be fine."

I was sure we were finished with that subject. That left me with little to do but try to enjoy the ride.

At 1800, the Marines were led in groups of twenty to the NCO mess for evening chow. Then they had a thirty-minute break on deck while the second group of twenty ate. By 2000, they were all back in their quarters.

I joined the eight commissioned officers in the officers' mess at 1900. Every space on a ship of that size was tight, and the officers' mess was no different. Seven officers in their duty khakis and me in my dress khakis sat across from one another at the mess table.

Commander Denton entered, and everyone stood. "As you were, gentlemen," came the standard gesture, and we all sat down. "Our guest at the end of the table is Lieutenant Gehweiler. He is escorting the Marines below deck back to Okinawa. Seems he was on the *Iwo Jima* for a while. Try to make him feel at home."

I noted his slight sarcasm and saw smiles cross the faces of a few of the ensigns seated around me. I looked up the table and gave a nod to those who made the effort to glance my way.

The ensign across from me extended his hand. "Bob Johansen. Welcome aboard."

I returned his handshake, which prompted two more ensigns to offer their hands and names as well.

Okay, now I feel a bit more comfortable, I thought.

The meal passed with light chatter about the trip to Okinawa and the details of the different departments each of the officers oversaw.

As we finished eating, Commander Denton addressed the officers. "Gentlemen, it looks like we're in for some rough weather. I want everyone to prepare your departments accordingly."

He stood, then we stood, and he departed. A few of the senior officers followed him. The others sat back down to finish their coffee.

I turned toward Ensign Johansen. "Weather?" I asked.

Smiles returned to the faces around me. One of the ensigns down the table spoke up. "You ain't scared of a little weather, are you, Lieutenant?"

I couldn't help myself. I looked straight at him and paused for a second. "The last time I can remember being scared was on Hill 818, when my helicopter got shot down. You ever been shot down?"

Dead silence.

I waited a second, then let him off the hook. "Relax, boys, I'm just screwin' with you." Then I reset the hook. "I did get shot down, but I wasn't scared until much later. Just show me where to puke when it gets rough."

I looked over at Johansen and gave him a wink. He smiled and sipped his coffee. Chairs pushed back as the rest of the crew slowly emptied.

Hell, I thought, *I'm pretty sure I didn't make any friends with that little exchange.* Oh well. I wasn't concerned about making lifelong friendships on a freaking four-day boat ride to Okinawa.

The weather began to turn nasty around 0500. The ship was obviously in heavy seas and rolling side to side enough that I had to hold myself in the bunk so I wouldn't be tossed out. I got up, dressed, and made my way toward the bridge to get a better idea of the situation.

A petty officer met me outside the door. "Best stay in your quarters right now, sir, until we get to daylight. You can't go out on the deck, and the commander is busy on the bridge."

Great. Well, back to the cell. The ship was really rolling side to side. I found some canvas webbing in the closet and realized it was meant to be attached to the bunk opening for just this occasion. In effect, I was strapping myself into the bunk. With no outside visual, it wasn't long before I began to feel nauseated.

15. Boat Ride from Hell

By 0700, I'd had enough. Bracing myself between the bunk and the table, I managed to get dressed again and stumble down the gangway to the officers' mess.

Three officers sat there drinking coffee as though nothing was happening. One was Johansen.

"Bob, how the hell do you deal with this crap?" I asked.

"With what?" He smiled.

Christ, I thought. *These are going to be four awfully long days.*

Wrong. These were going to be *eight* awfully long days.

Remember the LST's flat bow? Because the ship at times needed to discharge cargo on a beach, it had a flat bottom, with no keel. In heavy seas, the big metal behemoth crawled up the walls of waves and tended to roll to the port (left) as it made its way up. Once the bow crested the wave, the propellers came out of the water for a moment, causing the entire ship to shudder like a giant diving board before it careened down the back of the wave, rolling starboard (right) until it centered again just as its flat bow slammed into the wall of the next wave.

We spent the next three days corkscrewing, vibrating, and slamming into and over the waves of that Pacific storm until we lost one of the engines. With our speed diminished, the nightmare trip stretched to twice its normal duration.

I thought we were going to lose some of the Marines. After the second day of the storm, I had Gunny Thomas take me down to their quarters. I had to stop myself from retching when he opened the door. The smell was nearly unbearable. The toilets were overflowing. The decks were awash in vomit. The men lay in their bunks, holding on to anything they could to keep from being tossed to the floor.

I looked at Gunny Thomas. "This is bullshit. We need to do something. Get one of those petty officers down here with some hoses and wash down that floor. Get someone to clear the floor drains. Leave the door open so they can have some air."

"Lieutenant," he said, staring, "we've been doing just that every other hour since yesterday. If we leave the door open, the gas fumes from the trucks make it worse. Gunny Taylor and I are helping these guys in small groups up to a deck hatch for a breath of fresh air as often as we can. We're making sure they get as much water as they can handle, but it doesn't stay down long. We're just going to have to ride this out."

"Has the ship's doctor been down here?"

147

"Yes, sir. He's been tending to the worst as best he can. I have a detail going from rack to rack with water and cold towels." His once-sharp uniform looked as though it had been dipped in a sewer. In effect, it had.

"Son of a bitch!" It was all I could come up with. Pretty lame. I was getting a bit heated. With my voice rising, I said, "Look, Gunny, I know you got this, but I'm not used to feeling helpless. There has to be something I can do for you and these men."

For the first time, I saw his face mellow a bit. "Well, sir, you could always tell the captain to speed it up a bit." He paused. "Look, Lieutenant, if there was anything I needed, you'd be the first to know. If I do need something, I'll come find you."

He'd been kind, but I was dismissed. "All right, Gunny." I sighed loudly. "Make sure you do. Good luck."

I climbed back out of that hellhole and headed for the bridge. The bridge on an LST isn't much of a bridge, maybe only fifteen feet square. A petty officer was strapped to the helm (steering wheel) with the duty officer holding on to the rail behind the forward windows. A communications sailor was strapped into a chair in front of the communication equipment on the back wall. Another officer held on to a floor-to-ceiling support beam in the middle of the room.

"Permission to enter the bridge?" I asked as I stepped through the hatch.

The duty officer looked around briefly, then turned back to the window. "Permission granted."

As I stepped onto the bridge, I stared through the rain-streaked forward window. All I could see were huge, wind-whipped, white-capped rollers bearing down on us like freight trains. I felt a new respect for what those Navy guys did.

As the ship rolls side to side, the bridge feels the greatest degree of sway since it's at the highest point of the craft. Being atop the *Lyon County* felt like being perched at the top of a slow-moving metronome as it plunged into the depth of the trough below and then climbed up the next mountain. It was impossible to stand in one place. The roll was so severe that I, like the others not strapped to their stations, had to walk from one side of the bridge to the other and keep one foot against the wall to maintain our balance.

That absurd dance might have been comical if it weren't so demanding. Each crew served a four-hour shift—four hours of keeping the ship properly aligned against the rollers while dancing along. It required tremendous focus and stamina.

I'd come up to ask for any help I might get for the Marines. But it was clear that these men had their own problems. I stayed for only a few minutes and left without asking anything.

I spent the next four days either in my bunk or at the officers' mess eating crackers and sipping broth. I only left to check with Gunny Thomas.

Earlier in my life, I'd been in rough seas a few times on fishing boats. I'd never been bothered by seasickness. After that trip to Okinawa, I was never able to get out of sight of land without becoming sick as a dog. Hats off to the Navy boys. I knew it wasn't the life for me. I'd rather be in the air, with blue overhead and green below.

Finally, we limped into Okinawa. Medical vehicles awaited dockside to take the sickest men to the hospital.

I stood at the top of the gangway as Gunnery Sergeants Thomas and Taylor herded the survivors onto buses and headed for their next stop, which I hoped beyond hope included a long, hot shower and a clean bed for each of them. As I watched the buses load, I saw Gunnery Sergeant Thomas look up to where I stood. He straightened to attention and gave me a salute.

I returned it as sharply as I could. *You hard-ass Marine*, I thought. *I'm glad as hell to have met you.*

I spent the next month at Okinawa doing absolutely nothing other than awaiting orders to return stateside. I whiled away my time at the O Club and various less-than-reputable establishments in town.

• • •

On September 15, 1969, almost eleven months after I'd arrived in Vietnam, I boarded the big silver bird. American Airlines. Finally, I was going home.

The plane was loaded with men and women from all branches of the military. As we rolled down the runway and lifted off, a huge cheer filled the cabin. The hoots and hollers lasted for some time. Once at altitude, the stewardesses—and the liquor cart—were kept busy. Eventually, things calmed down and a quiet settled over the passengers. I'm sure many, like I did, began to reflect on their time in Vietnam and what returning home would be like. We'd soon learn it wasn't all we'd hoped for, nor expected.

16

Coming Home

We landed at LAX. I wore my Marine Corps dress green uniform with first lieutenant bars on my shoulders and two and a half rows of ribbons on my chest. Most were of no special note, common service ribbons and unit citations. But I was proud of the twenty-five air medals I'd earned, which denoted the 150 combat missions I'd been involved in. Twenty-five isn't a lot, really, but it did indicate I'd done my part.

I was feeling a bit proud and puffed up as I rode the escalator up to the main floor. That feeling quickly changed and would remain changed for a long time afterward. Some civilians coming down the opposite escalator began to hiss and scowl. A couple of boos rang out. I didn't know what to make of it.

During my tour, I had no idea about the opposition to the war back home. None of us did. We simply didn't get that news where we were. We woke up each day and did our job. We were consumed by flying and staying alive. We focused every day on what was directly in front of us. Home was a million miles away, and it was easier not to think about it than to worry about it.

As I crossed the terminal toward the baggage area, the negative reactions continued. The souvenir I'd chosen to carry with me probably didn't help—a Viet Cong AK-47. It seemed like a good idea at the time. Not so much now.

I managed to collect my bag and take a cab to my hotel. I'd fly out the next day to the East Coast and report to Marine Corps Air Station New River, in North Carolina.

I ate dinner that evening in the hotel restaurant with a few other Marines who also were headed out the next morning. Still dressed in our uniforms, we were the object of numerous steely stares and cold shoulders during our meal.

Our waitress, however, was kind. "Don't pay any attention to those jerks," I heard someone say in a slow, southern drawl. I looked up to see a beautiful blonde glide up to the table. "You men are heroes in my book. My brother's still over there, and I have all the respect in the world for you boys. What can I get you, gentlemen?"

"Well, you sure are a breath of fresh air, sweetheart," one of the Marines said. "You got a boyfriend, by any chance?"

Never leave a door open for a Marine in a situation like that. He'll absolutely walk through it.

A big smile crossed her face. She turned on the charm, batted her eyelids, and took another step forward. She stood right over the Marine and in her slow, sexy voice said, "As a matter of fact, I do, handsome. He's a Marine, too, but a little bigger than you."

Everyone at the table burst out laughing, even the Marine trying to get his foot out of his mouth.

We ordered our drinks and spent the rest of the meal discussing where each of us was headed. We all still had time left on our contracts with the Marine Corps. As an officer and pilot, I was committed for five years, and I had two and a half years left. Some of us would stay in and make it our career, and some would opt out. I would choose the latter.

The Marine Corps had been the best thing that ever happened to me. It made a man out of me. It gave me confidence, determination, and pride, qualities I'd rely upon my entire life. But out of necessity, the Marine Corps is a structured and strict environment. I already yearned for more freedom and flexibility. I wanted to find my own way. I wasn't sure what it was going to be, but I wanted to have the opportunity to find it and be successful in the private sector.

We finished our dinner and left our great waitress a huge tip. Then we said our goodbyes and headed for our rooms. We all had early flights. It had been a long trip home. I just hoped any further homecoming would be a bit more hospitable.

• • •

I spent the next two years at MCAS New River. A number of my buddies from Pensacola and Vietnam also were assigned there for the remainder of their commitments. They were attached to different helicopter squadrons, depending on the type of aircraft they'd been flying. Since there were no more H-34 squadrons, I was attached to base personnel—they had to find somewhere to stash me.

I was assigned to the flight-training department, which ran several flight simulators. The complicated, computer-driven simulators were used to hone flying skills in lieu of actually going up in the air. It saved time, money, and wear and tear on the aircraft. It also eliminated the possibility of aircraft accidents.

Was I qualified to run the simulators? Of course not. Luckily, I didn't have to be. The department was staffed by three staff sergeants, two gunnery sergeants, and a master gunnery sergeant. They were experts at it. My job was to stay the hell out of their way. I was in hog heaven. All I had to do was show up each morning and ask if they needed anything. They never did, so I'd shuffle some paperwork and exit the area by midday.

I also was required to maintain my flight hours. There were no H-34s around, and the Marine Corps wasn't going to waste time and money training me on another helicopter. However, the base did have two fixed-wing T-28s, which had been the basic trainer at Pensacola. It was like a dream come true. I loved that aircraft. It was more fun to fly than you can imagine. In essence, I had my own freaking airplane! I could fly anytime I wanted.

And I did. Flying up and down the beaches along the coast. Rolling around the mountainous cumulous clouds that filled the blue skies overhead. Snapping barrel rolls and wingovers and spins. My days were filled with the best flying any pilot could want.

At that time, Uncle Dick, my inspiration for entering the military, was president of the U.S. Naval War College in Newport, Rhode Island. He served there from 1968 to 1971. One day, I got a phone call.

An ensign from the War College was on the line. "Is this Lieutenant Gehweiler?"

"Yes, it is."

"Please hold for Admiral Colbert."

After a moment, I heard my uncle's voice. "Rick, how are you, son?"

"I'm fine, sir." I felt elated. "It sure is great to hear from you."

"What are you up to this weekend, Lieutenant?"

"Nothing that matters, sir."

"How about you fly up here tomorrow for a couple of days and watch the America's Cup with me?"

"That sounds fantastic, sir! I'll be there tomorrow. Thanks for asking. It will be great to see you again."

I grabbed one of the T-28s and flew up the next morning. I landed at Quonset Point Naval Air Station, about twenty miles north of the college. After I landed and taxied to the flight line, I watched a big black sedan pull up. It had two flags on the front bumper, each with three stars.

A Navy ensign popped out, saluted, and grabbed my bag. "Welcome, Lieutenant Gehweiler. The admiral is waiting at his quarters for you. Hop in."

It was a beautiful thirty-minute drive. First we went south along the crystal blue waters of Narragansett Bay, then we crossed via the Jamestown Bridge, over Conanicut Island, and then the Newport Bridge. As we crossed the latter bridge, before us appeared the spectacular setting of the Naval War College on a small peninsula that jutted into the bay.

As we drove through the gate, I marveled at the history of the beautiful and incredibly important institution, and what it meant to the free world. Established in 1884, the War College was intended to bring together the best and brightest naval officers from all countries in the free world. These officers would engage in a wide variety of courses and discussions and work to advance our communal knowledge toward a better world.

We proceeded toward the admiral's quarters, a gorgeous, three-story, colonial-style mansion known as the President's House. I was clearly out of my league, and more than a little nervous, especially because I was still dressed in my flight suit. Standing on the front steps was Uncle Dick, resplendent in his vice admiral's dress whites and ribbons galore.

The ensign opened the door for me. I stepped out and, for the second time in my life, was able to salute my uncle. He walked down the steps, and we gave each other a big hug.

"So good to see you, Rick," he said, holding me by the shoulders.

"It's great to see you too, sir." I struggled with my emotions. The last time I'd seen him was at my graduation at Quantico, just after my mother had died. Since then, Vietnam had come and gone, and I'd had little family contact. It was good to have that back, especially from someone whom I admired so much.

He motioned toward the house. "Let's get you inside so you can freshen up."

I grabbed my bag and turned toward the ensign. I glanced at his name tag and said, "Thanks, Ensign Evans. I enjoyed the ride."

I followed my uncle up the steps. We were met inside by a Filipino steward in starched whites, who showed me upstairs to my room.

I showered and changed into my dress khakis, making sure everything was perfect, especially my medals. I knew I'd be in some prestigious company the next two days, and I'd try my best to hold my own.

I found my way downstairs, and the same steward ushered me to a drawing room. Inside stood Uncle Dick, surrounded by six naval officers from other countries. Was I nervous? Oh yeah.

"Come here, Marine," Uncle Dick called. "I want to introduce you to a few of my friends."

Don't stumble, don't stumble, I thought as I walked over.

Uncle Dick began the introductions, which I immediately forgot. I remember there was an admiral from Venezuela and another from Italy. Those men were some of the brightest and most successful naval officers in the world. I was just a garden-variety lieutenant trying not to embarrass myself. They were great, though, and put me at ease immediately by telling me how proud my uncle was of my service in Vietnam, and how they shared his admiration.

Dinner was held at a long table with perhaps twenty guests, all senior naval officers from around the world. I'll always remember that night. They spoke of politics, the naval importance to world peace, and how the courses and interaction at the War College were so important to that end. It was more than educational. I knew from what I heard that there was a force in that room that could and would ensure that outcome. I had to pinch myself before going to bed that night to ensure I hadn't been dreaming.

♦ ♦ ♦

The plan for the next two days was to take out what was referred to as the Admiral's Barge and have a front-row seat to the America's Cup. Well, the "Barge" was anything but. At 9:00 a.m., eight of us walked down to the dock. There sat a beautiful, handcrafted, wooden, fifty-foot power yacht with a three-star flag fluttering on the bow. I learned years later that the yacht was a fixture at the War College for years and was used on special occasions to entertain dignitaries, including Dwight D. Eisenhower and John F. Kennedy.

We spent the next two days watching the sails of the America's Cup sloops plying the waters of Newport in quest of the coveted trophy. What a sight, what an experience, and what great memories.

After breakfast Monday morning with Uncle Dick and the same group of twenty officers, I said my goodbyes. Standing on the front step of the President's House, I told my uncle how much the experience meant to me, and how honored I was to be asked.

He smiled and put his hand on my chest, covering my medals. "You certainly earned it, Rick. Have a safe flight home, and don't forget to write now and then."

I stepped back and again had the pleasure of giving him a salute and watching him return it. "Yessir," I said. "Indeed, I will."

I turned and walked down the steps. Ensign Evans was waiting with the admiral's car to take me to my plane at Quonset. I pulled down my sunglasses so he couldn't see the moisture in my eyes. "I'm ready if you are, Ensign. What a hell of a weekend."

"I can only imagine." He smiled.

I spent the next two years at MCAS New River and was discharged from the Marine Corps on December 1, 1971.

17

You Can Run
but You Cannot Hide

The greatest tragedy of the Vietnam War was the treatment of veterans by the media and the general public. Referred to as criminals and "baby killers," veterans felt a sense of shock and despair upon their homecomings that would result in devastating, long-term damage for many.

Having endured hell on earth for months in Vietnam, the men and women of our military were treated to hell at home when they'd hoped for a grateful welcome and finally some peace of mind.

The Veterans Affairs system wasn't prepared to give us proper care. In many cases, wards in VA hospitals that were dedicated to the severely wounded were horribly understaffed, leaving patients no choice but to take care of one another. Given that the rate of amputees among wounded veterans was higher in Vietnam than in any other war, this was especially unforgivable.

In the early days of the war, post-traumatic stress disorder (PTSD) wasn't officially recognized. Treatment sometimes included barbaric electroshock therapy. Rather than try to treat this disease with counseling, some VA facilities saw fit to simply burn away the nightmares with electric jolts to the patient's brain. It was *One Flew Over the Cuckoo's Nest* in real life.

PTSD is an insidious and incurable disease. Like other disorders, it can be controlled, but it never goes away. We just have to learn to live with it. *We?*

Yes, I have PTSD. It took forty years for it to show up. That definitely accentuates the "post" part of the description, don't you think?

Suddenly, in certain situations, I became emotional at the drop of a hat. Like many veterans, I never talked about my experiences. There was no one in the civilian world who could understand them, even if I could explain everything. While we were all together in Vietnam, we didn't have to explain anything. We were all living it.

Given that in the days after we came home no one felt comfortable even being around a Vietnam vet, the subject of the war was pretty much taboo all around. That created the perfect scenario for stuffing everything in a pigeonhole in the back of your psyche. So that's what I did.

In 1992, my wonderful wife, Cheryl, and I were living in Bend, Oregon. We were out to dinner with friends one night. Someone asked if I'd been in the military.

"Yes, I was."

"What branch?"

"I was in the Marine Corps."

"Oh, wow. What did you do?"

"I was a helicopter pilot." I could feel something welling up inside of me.

"Did you serve in Vietnam?"

"Yes, I did." I was growing uncomfortable. I wasn't sure why, but I knew I had to keep my answers short.

"What was that like?" my friend asked.

That was it. My emotions came rolling out of some deep hole. Later in therapy, I'd describe the sensation as "puking emotion." I struggled to compose myself. It wasn't working. "Would you please excuse me for a minute?" I mumbled. I stood and made a beeline for the men's room. *What the fuck is happening to me?* I thought, staring into the mirror with tears streaming down my face. I turned on the tap and splashed cold water on my face. It wasn't enough, so I slapped myself. "Get it together, for God's sake," I said out loud. "What the fuck?" I splashed some more cold water on my face, took some deep breaths, and finally felt my come-to-Jesus moment.

When I returned to the dining room, the mood at the table was delicate and awkward.

"Sorry about that," I said. "I'm not sure where that came from. It's been a while since the subject came up, to be honest. I'm sorry if I embarrassed you. I do like the wine though. What do you guys think?" It was lame, but it was the best I could do.

As we headed home, Cheryl said, "Honey, you need to get some help about this."

There had been other incidents—road rage and short-temper reactions to minor issues. She'd noticed them, but I'd ignored them. The breakdown that night got my attention. It was embarrassing for me and Cheryl, and certainly the others at the table.

I went to the VA to see what could be done. That was one of the most difficult things I've ever done. I was a grown man. A Marine officer and a pilot. One of the top half of 1 percent of Americans able to say that. I'd always been in control. I was supposed to be strong, a tough guy. Being subject to such emotional weakness was humiliating.

Despite my misgivings, the office in Bend was great. After I filled out some forms, I was assigned to a counselor for an evaluation. During my first session, it became obvious to both of us that I had some serious underlying problems. When you can't have a normal conversation about your past without becoming emotional to the point of muteness, you definitely have a problem.

I was fortunate to be assigned to an incredible counselor. He was a godsend. His name will remain anonymous, but for this story, I'm going to call him Dr. Stephens. After four or five individual sessions, he suggested I was ready for group therapy.

"Okay, Doc, whatever you think."

One week later, I entered a room at the VA for my first group therapy session. There were about ten guys sitting around a table, with Dr. Stephens at the head. I had no idea how long these men had been part of this group, nor what their stories were.

Dr. Stephens began by asking each of us to introduce ourselves with a brief reference to our branch of service and our military occupation specialty code, as well as the years we served, and any short statement we wanted to make.

Each man's response was short and subdued, but full of pride. No one made any personal statements. The golden rule was not to talk about the incidents we experienced in Vietnam. No war stories, period. This was about solving the problems of our disease, not reviving memories.

"Jim Caruthers. D Company. 2/3 Marine Corps. 1968. Grunt."

"Fred Simmons. Corpsman, U.S. Navy. Attached to 3/4. 1969. Quang Tri."

There were no braver men in battle than Navy corpsmen. They were the Marine version of an Army medic. They'd hurl themselves into intense fire to save a wounded Marine regardless of risk. There isn't a

Marine alive who's seen combat and doesn't hold those men in the highest regard.

"Ted Stevens. 101st Airborne. Vietnam. 1968."

Enough said.

As the introductions continued and my turn drew near, I could feel myself tighten up. Then it was my turn. "Rick Gehweiler. United States Marine Corps. Helicopter pilot. 1969." It was all I could choke out. I was overcome with emotion and looked down at the table to compose myself as the room grew silent.

When I looked up, I saw the nods around the table telling me it was okay. There was a silent acknowledgment that we were all brothers in this new fight. In that moment, for the first time, I felt I'd come home.

What made our counselor so great was that he had PTSD himself. He understood the disease. He could teach us how we could cope with it. He'd been a Catholic priest at one time. His wife had been a nun. They'd taken a troubled man into their home to help him through his personal difficulties. One night, the man entered their bedroom and shot each of them in the chest. Dr. Stephens survived. His wife didn't.

There aren't many people who can hold the respect of a bunch of cranky, mean-ass, incorrigible Vietnam veterans. Dr. Stephens did. We knew that he knew. When he talked to us, we listened because we knew that he knew.

During one session, he drew a big letter *Y* on the blackboard. He explained that before we went to war, all of the friends we'd grown up with shared our same experiences—playing sports, going to movies, and dating girls. We were all similar. That period in our lives, Dr. Stephens said, is represented by the stem of the letter *Y*. Then some of us went to war. Our lives became drastically different. Our psyches were altered by what we experienced in war and combat. The friends we left at home are represented by the left-hand upper section of the *Y*. As we changed, we became the right-hand section. The difference between the sections would always remain. His job, he told us, was to teach us how to help lessen the gap.

He taught us that we had this disease, and we'd always have it. But it didn't have to rule our lives. There were ways to deal with it. He taught us how to deal with it. Those who used the tools he gave us definitely improved. I use these tools to this day.

For some, though, the disease was so deep, they couldn't make the tools work. For years after the war, suicide rates for Vietnam vets were significantly above general population rates. No wonder. Three of our group eventually made that unfortunate choice.

It took almost forty years for conditions to change. If anything good came from the Vietnam War experience, it's that eventually the American public came to realize how badly the Vietnam veteran was treated. Efforts began to reduce the risk that Marines, soldiers, and sailors returning from Iraq and Afghanistan would face the same experience. Some progress has been made, and although the VA system has improved to take care of those veterans who deserve everything this country has to offer, much more still needs to be done to address the problem.

There are still hundreds of thousands of men and women with PTSD as a result of their military service. We live with it, and we fight it on a daily basis.

Final Perspective

"It was the best of times; it was the worst of times..."

Those opening words of Charles Dickens's novel *A Tale of Two Cities* describe my year in Vietnam perfectly. Of course, there were tough times. Horribly tough. But the best of times came from the shared experience of flying with some of the best and bravest men I ever had the honor to know. While there were some dark days to be sure, there were good times and a lot of laughter. I still laugh out loud at the memory of "Hauser" stealing the ten-thousandth landing on the *Iwo Jima* from the squadron CO.

As odd as it may sound, I look back on it all as the highlight of my life. I was young and at the top of my game. The flying was incredibly demanding and extremely rewarding. The adrenaline was intoxicating. My job was to support my fellow Marines, and I took great pride in that. If I saved one life, it was more than worth it. I had a chance to do what few men did or will ever do. I look back on it often with a full measure of nostalgia.

When I talk with great Marine pals who shared those times, there's universal agreement regarding one question: If we could turn back the clock and had that choice, given all that happened, would we still do it again?

The answer is always the same: "IN A HEARTBEAT!"

God bless America, and God bless the United States Marine Corps.

Epilogue

Truth and Consequence

Volumes have been written about the Vietnam War. Every question, every perspective, and every opinion has been debated over and over again. But in my view, to understand the story of the Vietnam War, you need to consider only six questions.

1. How did the war begin?
2. How did the United States become involved?
3. Should the United States have become involved?
4. How did the United States lose the war?
5. What were the consequences of that loss?
6. What lessons did we learn?

Question #1: How did the war begin?

To gain a true perspective of how the war began, we need to look at the history of the area and what transpired to bring our country into what remains our most controversial military engagement.

Truth is based upon facts. I hope the facts below will shed some light on the truth.

- *1887*: France imposed a colonial system over Vietnam, calling it French Indochina. The system included Tonkin, Annam, Cochinchina, and Cambodia. Laos was added in 1893.
- *1923–1925*: Ho Chi Minh, a Vietnamese nationalist, trained in the Soviet Union as part of the Soviet International.
- *February 1930*: Ho Chi Minh, who was dedicated to a free and unified Vietnam, formed the Indochinese Communist Party in a meeting in Hong Kong.

Epilogue

- *September 1940*: As World War II broke out, Japan invaded Vietnam and defeated the French, who still occupied the area.
- *May 1941*: Ho Chi Minh established the League for Independence of Vietnam, known as the Viet Minh, the movement to resist both French and Japanese occupation of Vietnam.
- *March 1945*: Japanese troops occupying Indochina carried out a coup against French authorities and announced an end to the colonial era, declaring Vietnam, Laos, and Cambodia independent.
- *August 1945*: Japan was defeated by the Allies, leaving a power vacuum in Indochina. France began to reassert its authority over Vietnam.
- *September 1945*: Ho Chi Minh declared an independent North Vietnam and modeled his declaration on the American Declaration of Independence in an (unsuccessful) effort to win the support of the United States.

This is a salient point in the history of the area. China had tried to dominate and control Vietnam for centuries, resulting in centuries of military and expansionist conflicts. Its neighbor to the north had always been an enemy of Vietnam. So, when Ho Chi Minh declared an independent North Vietnam in September 1945, to whom did he look for support? Not China.

Ho Chi Minh looked for support from the United States. A June 1971 article from *The New York Times* states: "The *Christian Science Monitor* said today that the United States "ignored eight direct appeals for aid from the North Vietnamese Communist leader, Ho Chi Minh, in the first five winter months following the end of World War II."

The *Times* article continued quoting the *Christian Science Monitor*: "And, according to previously unpublished Pentagon papers, Ho also sent several messages through secret channels even earlier, in August and September of 1945, proposing that Vietnam be accorded the 'same status as the Philippines'—an undetermined period of tutelage preliminary to independence."

The Pentagon papers said Ho Chi Minh's reputation as a communist as well as Washington's determination to support France were fatal barriers to aid for the North Vietnamese leader, the *Monitor* reported, even though government analysts believed he possessed "real political strength."

The article again quoted the *Monitor*: "When Ho got no answers to his messages, sent between October 1945 and February 1946, he acquiesced in a return of the French to Vietnam for a five-year period."

Mr. Ho answered his Vietnamese critics by saying that in the face of two evils, he preferred to put up with the French for five years rather than the Chinese for the rest of his life, the story said.

So, there it is. Hindsight is always 20/20, much easier than trying to make the right decision in the moment. But it does beg the question of "what if?" But "what if?" never happened. The rest is history.

- *July 1946*: Ho Chi Minh rejected a French proposal granting Vietnam limited self-government, and the Viet Minh began a guerrilla war against the French.
- *June 1950*: The United States, identifying the Viet Minh as a communist threat, stepped up military assistance to France for its operations against the Viet Minh.
- *March–May 1954*: French troops were humiliated by Viet Minh forces at Dien Bien Phu. The defeat solidified the end of French rule in Indochina.
- *April 1954*: In a speech, U.S. president Dwight D. Eisenhower said the fall of French Indochina to communists could create a domino effect in Southeast Asia. This "domino theory," a premise derived from the prolonged Cold War and the perceived international threat from communism, guided U.S. thinking on Vietnam for a decade.
- *July 1954*: The Geneva Accords established North and South Vietnam, with the 17th parallel as the dividing line. This gave even more fuel to the desire of Ho Chi Minh and the Viet Minh to fight for a fully unified Vietnam.

Question #2: How did the United States become involved?

- *July 31, 1964*: In a continuing effort to help the South Vietnamese conduct secret military actions against the North, U.S.-backed patrol boats shelled two North Vietnamese islands.
- *August 2, 1964*: The USS *Maddox* was cruising offshore when the American destroyer was attacked by three North Vietnamese torpedo boats. The *Maddox* inflicted serious damage to one and sustained no damage itself.

Epilogue

- *August 3, 1964*: U.S.-backed patrol boats attacked two additional North Vietnamese defensive positions.
- *August 4, 1964*: Another American destroyer, the USS *Turner Joy*, joined the USS *Maddox* in the area. That night, the *Maddox* allegedly was attacked by North Vietnamese torpedo boats on patrol in the Gulf of Tonkin. The attack, which was later disputed, led President Johnson to call for air strikes on North Vietnamese patrol boat bases. Two U.S. aircraft were shot down, and one U.S. pilot, Everett Alvarez, Jr., became the first U.S. airman to be taken prisoner by North Vietnam.
- *August 1964*: The attacks in the Gulf of Tonkin spurred Congress to pass the Gulf of Tonkin Resolution, which authorized the president to "take all necessary measures, including the use of armed force" against any aggressor in the conflict.

What followed was a critical point in the history of the Vietnam War. An excerpt from history.com on the Gulf of Tonkin incident:

> Throughout these hectic few days, the Johnson administration asserted that the destroyers had been on routine patrol in international waters. In actuality, however, the destroyers were on an espionage mission in waters claimed by North Vietnam. The Johnson administration also described the two attacks as unprovoked; it never disclosed the covert US-backed raids taking place. Another problem: the second attack almost certainly never occurred. Instead, it's believed that the crewmembers of the Maddox mistook their own sonar's pings off the rudder for North Vietnamese torpedoes. In the confusion, the Maddox nearly fired at the Turner Joy. Yet when US intelligence officials presented the evidence to policy makers, they "deliberately" omitted most of the relevant communications intercepts, according to National Security Agency documents declassified in 2005. "The overwhelming body of reports, if used, would have told the story that no attack had happened," an NSA historian wrote. "So, a conscious effort ensued to demonstrate that an attack occurred." The Navy likewise says it is now "clear that North Vietnamese naval forces did not attack Maddox and Turner Joy that night.

So, the truth is that Lyndon Johnson and those who ascribed to the "domino theory" contrived a story to validate military action in Vietnam, and they lied to the American people about it.

Truth #1

The "domino theory" premise was incorrect, or else the communists that control Vietnam, with the support of other communist countries, would have marched down the Asian peninsula to Australia's front door. Of the twelve countries that comprise Southeast Asia today, only three are controlled by communist governments.

TRUTH #2

The Gulf of Tonkin incident, the basis for the Gulf of Tonkin Resolution, which gave President Johnson the authority to begin the war in Vietnam, was fabricated.

Question #3: Should the United States have become involved?

In my opinion, based on Truth #1 and Truth #2, the answer can only be NO.

Question #4: How did the United States lose the war?

How is it possible that the greatest military power on Earth was unable to defeat a weaker, smaller country when we had superior firepower, equipment, and total control of the skies?

Consider the following:

1. We were an invading force. The North Vietnamese were fighting on their own turf, and had been doing so for decades, if not centuries, if you consider their long conflicts with China. They were willing to fight as long as necessary and endure untold casualties and hardships to prevail.
2. The jungles of Vietnam were formidable. Trying to find an enemy that knew how to strike, then retreat and disappear into the jungle, made every operation difficult. The North Vietnamese had perfected this tactic in defeating the French.
3. It was the first guerrilla war for U.S. forces. We were used to taking territory and holding it. U.S. military strategy at the time was based on search-and-destroy tactics. Troops ventured out, tried to find, and engage the enemy, and retreat to secure bases. As a result, the United States never controlled the countryside. If you can't control the countryside, you can't control the country. If you can't control the country, you can't win the war.
4. The North Vietnamese wanted to win more than we did. U.S. politicians weren't willing to put forth the full effort necessary

165

Epilogue

for victory. North Vietnamese military leader General Vo Nguyen Giap knew he could outlast the American effort. He understood us and our history much better than we understood his.

5. The fact that politicians like Robert McNamara were running military operations rather than military experts with the necessary training, background, and expertise was a fatal mistake. McNamara's control of the type, location, and time of air strikes in the North was disastrous and caused untold damage to the overall effort. He later admitted this error.

6. The opinion of the war changed after the Tet Offensive. In particular, a broadcast by Walter Cronkite as he walked down the streets of Hue during that bloody battle set the tone, when he said that based on what he was witnessing, he didn't believe the war could be won. The problem is that Cronkite was only reporting on what he saw during that battle. He didn't fully understand what we were accomplishing. He simply didn't have all the facts to back up his conclusion. But he was a powerful figure, and his voice carried far and wide.

7. The American public couldn't stomach the reality of war. For the first time, images of its devastation and cruelty were broadcast nightly into American homes. The antiwar movement pushed by the media and figureheads like Jane Fonda and John Kerry put so much pressure on politicians that the beginning of the end soon was at hand.

The sentiment that America lost the war at home partially because of antiwar protests and media coverage was confirmed by Bui Tin, a former colonel in the North Vietnamese Army.

During a 1995 interview with the *Wall Street Journal*, when asked about the U.S. antiwar movement's impact, Tin replied:

It was essential to our strategy. Support of the war from our rear was completely secure while the American rear was vulnerable. Every day our leadership would listen to world news over the radio at 9:00 a.m. to follow the growth of the American antiwar movement. Visits to Hanoi by people like Jane Fonda, and former Attorney General Ramsey Clark and ministers gave us confidence that we should hold on in the face of battlefield reverses. We were elated when Jane Fonda, wearing a red Vietnamese dress, said at a press conference that she was ashamed of American actions in the war and that she would struggle along with us.

166

Epilogue

Perhaps one of the most prophetic quotes has been credited to the legendary North Vietnamese General Vo Nguyen Giap himself: "Do not fear the enemy, for they can take only your life. Fear the media more, for they will destroy your honor."

Consequences

By the end of the war, more than 58,000 Americans had lost their lives. More than 300,000 had been wounded, many severely. More than 1,600 remain missing. An estimated 500,000 suffered—and many still suffer from—debilitating PTSD.

Vietnam has released estimates that 1.1 million North Vietnamese and Viet Cong fighters were killed, up to 250,000 South Vietnamese soldiers died, and more than two million civilians lost their lives on both sides of the war.

U.S. prestige in the world suffered a severe setback as our "promise" to protect the South Vietnamese in their fight against the North proved hollow at best. In effect, we deserted them. It's estimated that after the fall of Saigon in 1975, more than 80,000 civilians lost their lives to reprisals by the North.

Lessons

What did we learn from the Vietnam War? I'm still not sure, but here are my observations, short and ... well, short.

1. Make sure the reason for going to war is based upon undeniable national interests and the strategic defense of this country. Vietnam was not.
2. Don't go to war unless you're prepared to do everything necessary to win. Half measures only sacrifice those willing to take on the challenge. They deserve the full force and effort this country can bring to bear. In Vietnam we did not.
3. For God's sake, take care of those men and women and their families when they come home. As for the Vietnam Veterans our country did not.

Military History
of Richard W. Gehweiler

After graduating from the University of North Carolina, Rick joined the United State Marine Corps, reporting to Officer Candidates School in Quantico, Virginia, in February of 1967. After ten weeks of training, he was commissioned as a Second Lieutenant and then reported to Marine Corps Air Station in Pensacola, Florida, for naval flight training. During the next fifty-eight weeks Rick would earn his Navy wings in the T-28 fixed wing aircraft and then go on to train as a helicopter pilot in the Bell-13 and finally the Sikorsky H-34 which he would eventually fly in Vietnam. In September of 1968 Rick reported to Marine Corps Air Station Santa Ana for advanced combat flight tactics.

By the end of October 1968 Rick was transferred to Vietnam and assigned to HMM 362 based at Marble Mountain just outside of Da Nang. He was in fact the last Marine pilot to be assigned to HMM 362 and the last pilot to be assigned to fly the H-34 in Vietnam, a noteworthy and proud footnote. Shortly thereafter HMM 362 was relocated to Phu Bai up nearer to the DMZ (Demilitarized Zone). The rest of his tour would be spent flying with HMM 362 out of Phu Bai, other than a two-month rotation with the squadron aboard the *Iwo Jima*, a helicopter carrier anchored off the coast of Vietnam near Da Nang.

His combat flying missions were a combination of resupply, medevacs, troop inserts and extracts. In August of 1969 HMM 362 was withdrawn from Vietnam and the old H-34 warhorse was decommissioned. Rick was transferred to Okinawa for the last two months of his thirteen-month tour of duty and subsequently reassigned to Marine Corps Air Station in New River North Carolina to serve out the last two years of his military commitment.

Since there were no more H-34 squadrons, Rick was assigned to base personal as Officer in Charge of the base flight simulators division. He was discharged on December 1, 1971.

During his Vietnam tour Rick earned the Vietnam Service Medal, the Vietnam Cross of Gallantry, the Vietnam Service Medal with two stars, the Merit Unit Citation, the Combat Action medal and twenty-five Air Medals.

Index

Index